THE
LOW-FODMAP
6-WEEK PLAN & COOKBOOK

A Step-by-Step Program of Recipes and Meal Plans

Alleviate IBS
and Digestive
Discomfort!

Suzanne Perazzini

FAIR WINDS

Brimming with creative inspiration, how-to projects, and useful information to enrich your everyday life, Quarto Knows is a favorite destination for those pursuing their interests and passions. Visit our site and dig deepe with our books into your area of interest: Quarto Creates, Quarto Cooks, Quarto Homes, Quarto Lives, Quarto Drives, Quarto Explo es, Quarto Gifts, or Quarto Kids.

First Published in 2018 by Fair Winds Press, an imprint of The Quarto Group,
100 Cummings Center, Suite 265-D, Beverly, MA 01915, USA.
T (978) 282-9590 F (978) 283-2742 QuartoKnows.com

Fair Winds Press titles are also available at discount for retail, wholesale, promotional, and bulk purchase. For details, contact the Special Sales Manager by email at specialsales@quarto.com or by mail at The Quarto Group, Attn: Special Sales Manager, 401 Second Avenue North, Suite 310, Minneapolis, MN 55401, USA.

22   21   20   19   18   1   2   3   4   5

ISBN: 978-1-59233-789-7
Library of Congress Cataloging-in-Publication Data is available

Design and Page Layout: Laura Shaw Design
Cover Image: Alison Bickel Photography
Photography: Alison Bickel Photography

Printed in China

The information in this book is for educational purposes only. It is not intended to replace the advice of a physician or medical practitioner. Please see your health-care provider before beginning any new health program.

This book is for you—the men, women, and children in the world who are suffering from any digestive disorder which interferes with your enjoyment of life. My greatest hope is that you use this book as your ultimate guide for controlling your symptoms and leading you to a joyful, inspired place where you can live life to its fullest.

Contents

Introduction

IBS. It's the bane of your existence. It's the enemy at the gates that never leaves you alone. It's the siege that saps your energy and drains your personal power. When you're battling IBS, you're at war—with yourself and your own body. You advance an inch, and then the enemy knocks you backward, keeping you in check—and keeping your life on hold.

But what if you could end this war? What if you were empowered to fight with determination; to find your way back to health; and to live a joyful, fulfilled life? Imagine if the following were true:

- You were pain-free: no bloating, diarrhea, or constipation.

- You had the knowledge to help you make healthy, low-FODMAP food choices.

- You'd developed a nutritionally-balanced diet that was tailor-made for your individual needs.

- You had the strength to stay the course into the future, having overcome the mental blocks that stood in your way.

- You had a new plan and a new set of habits that promoted a balanced lifestyle, to help support the diet's effects.

You might think this sounds too good to be true. But it isn't. This can be your reality—your new normal. And it starts when you decide to take your life and your health into your own hands, and you become proactive about getting well. The low-FODMAP diet has been scientifically proven—at research centers at Monash University in Melbourne, Australia, and the University of Michigan—to help eliminate symptoms in the majority of IBS sufferers. This program could be your savior.

Let me introduce myself: My name is Suzanne Perazzini. I'm a certified nutritional therapist, and I've suffered from irritable bowel syndrome (IBS) all my life. I've always been obsessed with finding the location of the nearest toilet—one of the first signs of potential IBS—and I spent decades turning down invitations that might expose my secret because IBS is a secret affliction that sufferers keep well hidden. After all, discussions of bowel functions don't make for polite conversation!

Over the years, I bounced from health practitioner to health practitioner without finding any definitive answers. But with the advent of the Internet, I started to do my own research. I Googled my symptoms over and over again until the information available on the Internet caught up with my needs, and eventually, I learned about the low-FODMAP diet.

At first, I ignored the diet. It was so complicated, and it seemed almost impossible to understand: FODMAPs are found in nearly all foods, so if we eliminated all foods containing them, we'd die from malnutrition. And so I kept ignoring it. But one day, I was desperate enough to stop and read about the diet a little more closely. That's when it all fell into place. My symptoms were all there. I concluded that I had IBS and that the low-FODMAP diet was the answer.

Thus began a period of intensive research and experimentation. There was only a limited amount of information on the diet available on the Internet at that time, and much of it was conflicting. Still, even though it took about a year to assemble the many moving parts of the diet and to eliminate all my symptoms, I knew I was onto something, so I persevered through all the hiccups and disappointments while I figured it out.

Let's fast-forward to the present day. My life has now been completely revolutionized by the low-FODMAP diet and by the other lifestyle changes I've made to support my health. Plus, I'm now a certified nutritional therapist and trained teacher: I coach IBS sufferers on how to implement this fabulous-but-complicated low-FODMAP diet in their own lives. I also teach them how to remove or reduce other gut irritants and how to make the necessary lifestyle changes to minimize the symptoms of their IBS. Every day I help people from all over the world become well so that they can finally be free from the impossibly heavy burden of IBS.

This book contains all the knowledge I've accumulated over several years of living on the diet. It also includes everything I've learned from the hundreds of coaching clients I've helped, as well as the substantial research I've conducted and the many in-depth courses I've taken on the digestive system and the gut microbiome.

The first section explains IBS and the low-FODMAP diet. The second section is the exact program I use with my coaching clients. It consists of daily meal plans, recipes, a diary page for recording vital information, a weekly exercise to help you establish a balanced lifestyle to manage your IBS, and a weekly section on integrating the diet into your everyday life. Each week ends with a case study to inspire you to dig deep and to help you stay the course.

This will be an exciting journey toward a life free from pain and embarrassment. You're about to embark on the ride of your life—so hold on tight!

PART 1

FODMAPS AND THE LOW-FODMAP DIET

CHAPTER 1 Understanding IBS

Irritable bowel syndrome (IBS) is a common chronic disorder that involves the large intestine and causes bloating, abdominal pain, constipation, and/or diarrhea. Unfortunately, its exact cause is still unknown, but scientists currently believe that visceral hypersensitivity—that is, a highly-sensitive intestinal tract—reacts to the normal distension of the gut by changing motility patterns and sending messages to the brain that may be misinterpreted. This makes the intestines contract or spasm in an abnormal way, causing pain. These contractions can either speed up the passage of matter through the bowel, resulting in diarrhea, or it can slow it down, resulting in constipation. The low-FODMAP diet reduces fermentation in the gut, thereby decreasing gas production, minimizing the distension of the bowel, and therefore reducing symptoms.

Other factors may play a part in IBS, too. Research is underway on the gut microbiome—the collection of microbes or microorganisms that inhabit the digestive system—and it may play a part in the IBS puzzle. The effect of food chemical intolerance is also being investigated. Such chemicals may stimulate nerve endings in hypersensitive people, including those with IBS, resulting in pain and other symptoms. This research is ongoing, and scientists have yet to confirm whether eliminating food chemicals could help reduce IBS symptoms.

Still, scientists have identified a number of possible IBS triggers. They include the following:

INHERITED GENES

A number of studies—including a 2008 study published in *Neurogastroenterology & Motility* and a 2010 study published in the *Journal of Pediatric Gastroenterology and Nutrition*—have shown that the chances of contracting IBS are higher in the sibling or child of an IBS sufferer. Both male and female relatives of a person with IBS are two to three times more likely to have it, too. Still, it is not clear whether this is due to hereditary or environmental factors.

STRESS

As a study published in 2000 in *Gut*, a leading international journal in gastroenterology and hepatology, has demonstrated, stress plays a large part in triggering or aggravating symptoms. Psychological factors affect the link between the brain and the gut, and nerve signals can be misinterpreted by the brain.

AN INFECTION IN THE DIGESTIVE SYSTEM

A 2007 review in *Alimentary Pharmacology & Therapeutics* showed that the risk of developing IBS increases six-fold after a gut infection accompanied by severe diarrhea, and this risk remains elevated for at least two to three years. Scientists' understanding of the pathophysiology of post-infectious irritable bowel syndrome remains limited and requires further research, but the good news is that the symptoms of this type of IBS may be eradicated completely. (With other types of IBS, symptoms can be controlled, but will never completely disappear.)

WHAT ARE THE SYMPTOMS OF IBS?

There are a few common symptoms of IBS. They include the following:

BLOATING

In healthy people, FODMAPs are absorbed through the lining of the small intestine. When an individual has difficulty with this, the FODMAPs pass to the large intestine, where the resident bacteria cause them to ferment. This fermentation produces hydrogen or methane, which accumulates in "pockets" instead of being distributed throughout the colon—and this, in turn, causes bloating.

DIARRHEA AND/OR CONSTIPATION

Diarrhea is caused either when an excess of liquid enters the bowel or when food moves through the bowel too quickly for the water in the food to be absorbed. This "drying-out" mechanism may also be hindered by inflammation of the colon. Constipation, on the other hand, is caused either by a lack of liquid in the bowel, or when the matter in the bowel becomes too dry because the contents of the bowel are moving too slowly or because you haven't gone to the toilet as soon as you feel the urge. Diarrhea and constipation aren't mutually exclusive; some IBS sufferers swing back and forth between both.

PAIN/CRAMPING

In a person with IBS, the digestive system is hypersensitive, and it overreacts to stimuli such as high-FODMAP foods, fiber, fat, and stress levels (to name just a few). This results in painful cramping as the wrong foods make their way through the gut. While excess fermentation in the bowel of a healthy person goes relatively unnoticed, the IBS sufferer perceives it as pain because of the faulty brain-to-gut connection mentioned previously.

LACK OF ENERGY

As long as you've had IBS, you have been malnourished because your intestines have not been properly absorbing nutrients from the food you eat, no matter how "healthy" your diet has been. After all, the simple act of eating is no guarantee that your body will be well-nourished. If much of the food you eat bypasses the small intestine and moves directly into the bowel, then it's almost as if you haven't eaten at all, as far as nutrients are concerned. That's why you'll notice a marked improvement in your energy levels very soon after commencing an accurate low-FODMAP diet.

HOW IS IBS DIAGNOSED?

IBS is a diagnosis of exclusion. The first step is to visit a gastroenterologist who will test you for all other possibilities, such as inflammatory bowel diseases including Crohn's disease and colitis; small intestinal bacterial overgrowth (SIBO); and—as a worst-case scenario—cancer. This will involve, at the very least, blood tests, stool tests, and a colonoscopy.

If all the tests come back negative but the symptoms persist, then a diagnosis of IBS is made. At that point, your health practitioner will offer you medication to mask the problem and will (hopefully) tell you about the low-FODMAP diet. In many instances, though, this involves simply being told to look it up on the Internet and/or being given a list of foods to avoid. Food lists are just the tip of the iceberg when it comes to this complicated (but life-changing!) diet, as you'll find as you continue to read this book.

TRIGGERS FOR IBS SYMPTOMS

Let's have a look at some of the triggers of IBS, apart from high-FODMAP foods.

CARBONATED DRINKS

The bubbles in carbonated drinks are a gut irritant because they introduce gas into the gut. They also present another problem: their sugar levels. Sweetened carbonated drinks have much more sugar than an IBS sufferer can tolerate. "Diet" drinks are to be avoided, too, even though they sometimes use low-FODMAP sweeteners, such as aspartame. The drawbacks of such artificial sugars—including headaches and digestive issues—have been well documented. The safest carbonated drink is plain soda water, and that should be enjoyed only as an occasional treat because it'll still introduce gas into the gut.

LARGE MEALS

Large meals can stimulate the hormones involved in the gastrocolic reflex (an increase in colonic motility or movement triggered by eating). This, in turn, triggers colon contractions, which can cause painful gut cramps. Later on in this book, I'll show you how to eat smaller meals, more often, leaving at least three hours between each.

SKIPPING MEALS

IBS sufferers are often tempted to skip meals, believing that this will reduce symptoms. This isn't a good idea, though, because the goal is regularity. Help your digestive system learn to operate efficiently by eating five smaller, more frequent meals according to a well-structured routine. There is also the possibility that gas may start to accumulate in the gut once digestion has finished, and more gas is the last thing we need.

LACK OF LIQUID

Drinking water during meals was once thought to dilute your digestive juices, but this isn't so. It's important to drink six to eight glasses of plain water a day. According to the latest research, you should sip water slowly during your meal: It'll help the passage of food through the gut. Not drinking enough water will aggravate the symptoms of IBS sufferers with constipation.

MEDICATION

Some drugs can trigger spasms of the colon, and these spasms can lead to constipation or diarrhea. Some common culprits include the following:

- Antibiotics, especially after prolonged use

- Medicine containing sorbitol, such as cough syrup

- Supplements that contain high-FODMAP nonactive ingredients

- Certain antidepressants—especially older antidepressants called tricyclic antidepressants—can cause constipation. Standard antidepressants (called selective serotonin reuptake inhibitors, which include Prozac and Zoloft) can cause diarrhea, at least initially. Your doctor can help you find an antidepressant that won't aggravate your IBS symptoms.

MENSTRUATION

Studies show that women with IBS tend to experience worse symptoms during their periods (see page 15). Consult your health practitioner about using certain oral contraceptives and premenstrual dysphoric disorder (PMDD) drugs to ease discomfort. Drugs used to treat depression, such as Sarafem, Paxil CR, and Zoloft, may also help. They adjust the brain's levels of serotonin, which is a chemical that may be out of balance during segments of a woman's cycle.

FIBER

Fiber is a gut irritant, but we do need it for "normal" bowel function. Around 1 ounce (28 grams) is the recommended fiber intake for the general population. As an IBS sufferer, you may need less in order to prevent fiber-induced symptoms. The exact amount of fiber you should consume is highly individual, and trial and error is the only way to find out what works for you. It's a fine balance, but it's important to experiment in order to get as much fiber into your diet as possible without triggering your symptoms.

The following are good sources of fiber:

- All fruits and vegetables—keeping the skins of fruit and vegetables on increases the amount of fiber even more. Spread your fruit and vegetable intake throughout your five small daily meals so that you're not eating too much fiber in a single meal.

- Nuts. Try to eat some low-FODMAP nuts each day.

- All grains—some, such as oats, brown rice, oat or rice bran, and quinoa have more fiber than others.

- Chickpeas and lentils—¼ cup (42 g) canned chickpeas, drained, and ½ cup (99 g) canned lentils, drained.

You can easily get adequate fiber from eating fresh, unprocessed foods. Avoid fiber supplements; they are too fierce and can aggravate your symptoms.

FAT

Fat is a gut irritant due to its ability to increase colonic hypersensitivity. All the cells in our bodies require fat, so we can't cut it out of our diets completely. You need to eat enough fat to stay healthy and feel well, without triggering your symptoms. It's a fine line and, as with fiber, the tolerable level will be different for each individual. You have to find out where that line is for you. For instance, a drizzle of olive oil on a small salad might be okay, but perhaps deep-fried chips or french fries won't be. Also, if you have had your gallbladder removed, then you'll have to eat a lower-fat diet than most people.

Consuming too little dietary fat can aggravate constipation, so do get as much as possible within your individual limits.

HOW TO DEAL WITH AN IBS EPISODE

Dealing with an urgent IBS attack can be very upsetting. Where is the nearest bathroom? Will anyone else realize what is happening? This kind of pain and panic about the possibility of having an accident is no fun, and it can certainly be distressing.

DURING THE ATTACK

The most important thing is to stay calm, as hard as that may be, because stress plays a major role in exacerbating your symptoms. Slow, deep breathing works well because it reassures your body's emergency response system that there is no emergency. This will help interrupt those alarm signals that your brain is sending to your gut.

SELF-TALK

Talk to yourself calmly, as if you were a friend who is terribly upset and whom you need to help calm down. This will shift your panicked thought processes from high gear into a more relaxed, tranquil place. Start moving toward the toilet, knowing that your body is actually pretty good at holding things in. The calmer you are, the better it'll be able to do its job.

USE A HEATING PAD

From a purely psychological point of view, using a heating pad can be calming. Plus, research—including a study published in 2003 in the *Archives of Physical Medicine and Rehabilitation*—supports the use of low-level continuous heat as a way to speed up pain relief. Heat helps to relax the muscles in your gut and helps prevent pain sensations.

MAKE A CUP OF HERBAL TEA

Like a heating pad, there's something comforting about a nice cup of tea. Both of the following types of tea have a reputation for calming digestive distress and have gas-reducing reputations:

- Peppermint tea (This is not recommended for those with reflux.)

- Ginger and lemon (Be sure to check the packet for high-FODMAP ingredients.)

DON'T HOLD ON

Now is not the time to be bashful where passing wind is concerned. If at all possible, find a private place and let it rip. When intestinal gas has passed, there's less in your system to cause pain.

IF POSSIBLE, PASS A MOTION

If you are able to have a bowel motion, the movement of the muscles lining your large intestine will increase, which will help release the gas from your gut. A bowel movement also clears the passage, allowing the trapped gas to escape.

MOVE YOUR BODY

Gentle exercise is a practical option. Walking can help relax the muscles in your abdomen and allow gas to escape. If you have the space and the privacy, there are several yoga poses that may help ease the passage of intestinal gas, including happy baby pose (Ananda Balasana), wind-relieving pose (Pavanamuktasana), and gate pose (Parighasana).

AFTER THE ATTACK

Afterwards, you'll feel hypersensitive to any signals that may herald another attack. So take an even closer look at your diet and stay extra-vigilant about what you put in your mouth. No more mistakes! While your body is returning to normal, eat comfort foods such as rice, mashed potato, and plain chicken breast.

CONNECTED HEALTH ISSUES

IBS is, unfortunately, often accompanied by other health issues that can affect your quality of life. Here's a rundown of how to address the most common ones.

DEPRESSION/ANXIETY

Studies show that anywhere from 50 to 90 percent of people who seek treatment for IBS also suffer from some form of psychiatric disorder, such as panic disorders, anxiety, and major depressive disorder. Simply having IBS can be pretty depressing in itself, but these disorders may have a common physical cause, too. People with IBS have difficulty absorbing tryptophan, an amino acid. An important by-product of tryptophan is 5HTP (5-hydroxytryptophan), which increases the production of serotonin, one of the body's main mood-regulating hormones. As you start absorbing the nutrients from the foods you eat on the low-FODMAP diet, your mood levels should gradually improve. You may eventually—with your health practitioner's blessing, of course—be able to stop taking your antidepressants (unless there is another cause for your depression).

Plus, a study presented at the 22nd United European Gastroenterology Week in Vienna, Austria, demonstrated that patients with IBS have more difficulty suppressing pain signals coming from the bowel and that depression plays a role in this. Therefore, doctors may prescribe low doses of antidepressants to patients who don't have depression because those particular drugs may help block the brain's perception of pain. This may be due to the effect of the antidepressant on serotonin and other neurotransmitters. Tricyclic antidepressants, such as nortriptyline (Pamelor) and amitriptyline (Elavil), work by slowing down the intestinal tract, possibly making them the better choice for patients who have IBS with diarrhea.

Selective serotonin reuptake inhibitors, such as paroxetine (Paxil) or sertraline (Zoloft), are thought to target serotonin only, resulting in fewer unwanted side effects like constipation. For this reason, a person with IBS with constipation may feel better when using these sorts of antidepressants.

FIBROMYALGIA

Fibromyalgia presents as chronic widespread pain, and it can also include symptoms such as fatigue, sleep disturbance, joint stiffness, and depression. It affects 2 to 8 percent of the population, and a large majority of sufferers are women. Scientists still don't know exactly what causes it. The brains of fibromyalgia patients do show structural differences from the rest of the population, but scientists don't know whether the brain differences cause the symptoms or whether they stem from an underlying condition. Fibromyalgia is a chronic, possibly lifelong condition. The good news is that it is never fatal, and it will not cause damage to the body. If you suffer from fibromyalgia, visit a pain clinic that has experience in treating people with it.

HYPOTHYROIDISM

This is a condition in which the body doesn't produce enough of the thyroid hormone, which controls the body's metabolism. It's a common condition and affects around 10 percent of women.

There are two main causes of hypothyroidism. The first is inflammation of the thyroid gland. The inflammation damages the thyroid and prevents it from producing enough of the hormone. This can happen when a person's immune system causes the inflammation (Hashimoto's thyroiditis). The second cause is when a necessary surgical procedure requires removal of part or all of the thyroid gland—in instances of thyroid cancer, for example. Whether this causes hypothyroidism depends on how much of the gland is left and whether or not it can cope with the body's demands.

Symptoms of hypothyroidism include fatigue, weakness, weight gain, dry skin and hair, hair loss, feeling cold, muscle cramps, constipation, depression, irritability, and memory loss. In many patients, it's highly treatable and can be controlled with daily medication, but tailoring treatment to the individual may be slightly complicated at first. While research has not yet shown a direct correlation between IBS and hypothyroidism, many people with IBS suffer from hypothyroidism as well.

DIVERTICULOSIS

This condition develops when tiny pouches are formed in the wall of the colon. Scientists don't fully understand why this happens, but they suspect that a buildup of pressure—perhaps due to a lack of dietary fiber—against a weak part of the colon wall could be the cause. These pouches don't cause any problems in themselves, and many people don't even know they have them unless a colonoscopy reveals them. Only 20 percent of people with diverticulosis will contract diverticulitis, which occurs when the pouches become infected, and this requires treatment.

HEADACHES

A statistically significant link between migraine headaches and IBS exists. A 2005 study published in the *Polish Journal of Neurology and Neurosurgery* found that 23 to 53 percent of people with IBS experience frequent headaches. A study published in *Current Pain and Headache Reports* in 2012 revealed a further link between migraine headaches and IBS. Researchers traced the connection to a genetically sensitive nervous system which can gradually lead to chronic pain diseases, such as IBS and migraine headaches. Fortunately, controlling your IBS can also help reduce your migraines because the triggers are often the same—inadequate sleep, high stress, and an unhealthy diet.

REFLUX

Almost 80 percent of people with IBS could have reflux, and scientists think the mechanism is the same in both conditions. When acid constantly travels from the stomach to the esophagus, the result isn't just the unpleasant symptoms of reflux—there is also an increased risk of esophageal cancer, so you need to address it right away. Unfortunately, the antacids that are often prescribed by doctors lower the acid levels in the stomach, which can aggravate your IBS. So, the best solution is to layer a reflux diet over the low-FODMAP diet. This works efficiently to eliminate reflux symptoms— unless you have an underlying condition involving the sphincter muscle, which should prevent the acid from reentering the esophagus. A reflux diet means cutting out acidic foods, such as tomatoes, pineapple, citrus fruit, and bell peppers. Too much dietary fat, caffeine, and alcohol can also cause reflux, so you must limit the amounts you consume. (This will help your IBS symptoms, too.)

HOW HORMONES AFFECT IBS

The hormones in your body can also affect your IBS symptoms. Here's how:

SEX HORMONES

If you are a woman, you may have noticed that your IBS symptoms are worse before and during your periods. This is due to hormonal fluctuations. During the second half of your cycle, estrogen levels are lower for several days, but at the end of your cycle, progesterone levels are relatively high before dropping off suddenly just before your period. All women experience some changes in intestinal symptoms during their periods, but those with IBS feel these changes more acutely due to their hypersensitive systems. In general, women with IBS seem to suffer more from menstrual symptoms, such as water retention and concentration difficulties, in comparison to other women. Bloating also seems to be worse in the second half of the cycle, just before menstruation, in women with IBS.

GUT HORMONES

There is some evidence that IBS symptoms could be caused by abnormal activity in some of the gut hormones, especially after eating. In a couple of studies, these hormones have been shown to be higher in people with IBS. One study has shown that one of these hormones, motilin, increases in IBS sufferers when they're under stress. Therefore, abnormal behavior of these gut hormones in people with IBS is thought to play a part both in symptoms that occur after eating and symptoms that occur due to stress.

ADRENAL HORMONES

Many studies have demonstrated the negative effect of stress on IBS. The adrenal hormone cortisol produces many of the physical changes caused by stress, and two studies—published in 1996 in the *American Journal of Gastroenterology* and in 2001 in the *Journal of Endocrinological Investigation*— have reported that cortisol is unusually high in women with IBS.

The corticotropin-releasing hormone may also play a part. One Japanese research study published in 1998 reported that the intestines of IBS patients show stronger and longer-lasting muscle contractions in response to this hormone compared to control subjects.

In the next chapter, you'll learn exactly what FODMAPs are and why controlling your intake can significantly help reduce your IBS symptoms.

CHAPTER 2

The Low-FODMAP Diet

Now that you know how IBS presents and what some of its probable causes are, you might be wondering what FODMAPs are and what they have to do with IBS. FODMAPs are short-chain carbohydrates that are poorly absorbed by the small intestine. They're found in a wide range of foods. FODMAP is an acronym, and here's what each letter stands for:

F = Fermentable Fermentation occurs when carbohydrates that haven't been digested in the small intestine move down into the large intestine where they are fermented by the resident bacteria.

O = Oligosaccharides are carbohydrates, or sugars, which have two subgroups: fructo-oligosaccharides (FOS) or fructans found in wheat, rye, onions, and garlic, to name a few; and galacto-oligosaccharides (GOS) found in legumes, pulses (such as lentils), some vegetables, and some nuts.

D = Disaccharides are also a type of sugar. Lactose, found in milk and milk products such as soft cheese and yogurt, is a disaccharide.

M = Monosaccharides are simple sugars such as fructose. Fructose is found in most honeys, many fruits (mangoes and apples, for example), some vegetables (asparagus and sugar snap peas, for example), and high-fructose corn syrups.

A = And

P = Polyols are the sugar polyols (such as sorbitol and mannitol) found in some fruit and vegetables. They're also used as artificial sweeteners.

Not everyone responds to all of these compounds in the same way. For instance, 45 percent of people with FODMAP issues malabsorb fructose (that is they absorb it poorly), while only 25 percent malabsorb lactose. Fifty-seven percent malabsorb sorbitol, and 20 percent malabsorb mannitol.

Everyone malabsorbs fructans and GOS to some degree—even people with no FODMAP issues.

Thus, you may find that you have problems with some high-FODMAP foods, but not all of them. (You'll find out whether this is the case during the reintroduction stage of the diet in week four.)

HISTORY OF THE LOW-FODMAP DIET

Researchers at Monash University, led by Peter Gibson, M.D., carried out the first research study to show that a low-FODMAP diet improves IBS symptoms. In 2005, they published the first paper describing FODMAPs; then in 2006, the first research trial, confirming the role of a low-FODMAP diet in managing gastrointestinal complaints, was carried out at the university. Seventy-four percent of patients reported improvement in their symptoms on the diet. A randomized, placebo-controlled rechallenge trial in patients with IBS with fructose malabsorption took place in 2008 and confirmed the effectiveness of the diet. All patients improved, with their symptoms worsening significantly when fructose and/or fructans were reintroduced.

In 2011, a British study published in *Pharmaeconomics* showed that the low-FODMAP diet was superior to any previous dietary approach to treating IBS. Finally, in 2016, researchers at the University of Michigan also carried out a study on the low-FODMAP diet and came to similar conclusions to the Monash University study: At four weeks, the proportion of patients with a meaningful improvement in IBS quality of life was significantly higher in the low-FODMAP group compared to the control group (61 percent versus 27 percent).

THE STRUCTURE OF THE LOW-FODMAP DIET

The diet has two main stages: the elimination stage and the reintroduction stage.

THE ELIMINATION STAGE

During the elimination stage, you remove all foods that have high and moderate levels of FODMAPs from your diet. This creates a symptom-free baseline. You will build on this baseline during the reintroduction stage of the diet.

FODMAPs occur naturally in many of the foods that are necessary to a balanced diet, and you can't cut out all foods containing them from your diet. In the elimination stage, you start by eating only low-FODMAP foods in very specific amounts and in combinations with certain other foods.

How long the elimination stage lasts depends on how dedicated you are to sticking to the diet and on whether a secondary issue—such as gallbladder issues, inflammatory bowel disease, or SIBO—is causing problems as well. Your symptoms may disappear in as little as a couple of days, but it could take longer, depending on your reactions to other gut irritants, such as fiber, fat, caffeine, and alcohol, as well as any individual personal intolerances.

Even if your symptoms disappear very quickly, it's prudent to wait until a symptom-free week has elapsed before you begin to reintroduce foods. The duration of the elimination stage does depend on the individual, but it's best to remain on it for no longer than six weeks. Elimination removes many of the necessary prebiotics—indigestible plant fiber which helps regulate the gut bacteria—from your diet.

You may wonder whether you have the willpower to stick to such a strict diet, and yes, it will require a certain level of organization, plus lots of support from your family and friends. You'll have to keep your eye on the prize to avoid any lapses, but the rewards you experience should motivate you. You'll finally start to feel better—possibly for the first time in a very long time!

Remember that each IBS sufferer is different, even when it comes to following a low-FODMAP diet. You may be unlucky enough to malabsorb all high-FODMAP foods, but it's highly likely that you'll be able to eat many of them without experiencing symptoms. You'll discover your personal tolerance levels for these foods during the reintroduction stage.

THE REINTRODUCTION STAGE

During this stage, you'll discover your major triggers, your minor triggers, and the foods and groups that don't cause you any symptoms at all. This is an exciting but nerve-wracking time, so it's important that you're psychologically ready for it. There is no shortcut for this process, and the end result is worth the pain you may encounter when a major trigger is hit. You'll find out detailed instructions on how to carry out the reintroduction process in week four (page 118). Once this stage is complete, you'll have created the perfect custom-made diet for you as an individual. This will become the diet you follow throughout your life, and it will keep you symptom-free. Finally, your IBS won't control you: you'll control it!

In the next chapter, we'll talk about how to set yourself up for success when you're embarking on a low-FODMAP diet.

CHAPTER 3

Plan to Succeed

You're committed to following a low-FODMAP eating plan and to living a life free from the symptoms of IBS. That's great! This chapter will help you form healthy habits that'll maximize your chances of success.

SPACING OF MEALS

In chapter 1, you learned that it's important to avoid eating large meals on a low-FODMAP diet. For best results, you must eat five small meals three to four hours apart, so you'll need to work out a schedule that suits your lifestyle. It may look something like this:

Breakfast: 7 a.m.

Snack: 10 a.m.

Lunch: 1 p.m.

Snack: 4 p.m.

Dinner: 7 p.m.

Bedtime: At least three hours after eating dinner

Here's why a routine is so important. We need to leave approximately three hours between meals in order for a cleansing wave to pass through our digestive systems. A cleansing wave occurs when the muscles in the small intestine create a wave of forward motion in order to clean it out and to prevent matter from remaining in it. If we wait much longer than three hours, we start to accumulate gas in our intestines, which, in turn, can cause symptoms. So, you'll have to schedule your meals—and then schedule the rest of your life. After all, our bodies love routines, especially when it comes to life's basics, like eating, visits to the toilet, and sleep. We function much better when healthy routines are in place. Make sure you record your mealtimes on your diary pages so you can see if you are following your schedule.

FIRST-WEEK ADJUSTMENTS

In the first week of the diet, your body will be adjusting to eating in a healthier way (for your IBS, that is), so sometimes you'll feel hungry or full at inappropriate times. This is because your body is confused. By the second week, your body will have figured things out; your gut will have adjusted to the new eating plan, and these feelings should decrease.

BREAKFAST

Breakfast literally means breaking your nighttime fast, and that's what you must do within thirty minutes of rising. Your IBS body hates fasting at any time except during sleep: so, if you don't eat immediately, your gut can start to accumulate gas pockets, which cause bloating and pain.

BALANCED MEALS

For sufficient energy, you need to combine carbohydrates and protein at each meal. Carbohydrates supply energy quickly, but it doesn't last long. Energy from protein is metabolized slowly, but lasts longer. Together, they keep hunger at bay until your next meal. Make sure all five of your meals include protein, a grain (such as rice or quinoa) or starchy vegetable (such as potatoes or turnips), and a non-starchy vegetable (such as spinach, zucchini or radishes). That should keep your energy levels constant.

COMBINING FODMAPS

It's really important to follow the meal plans when combining foods. Why? It's like adding two and two and getting four. If you combine two foods from the same FODMAP category in the same meal, you end up with a double load of FODMAPs. So for example, if you're consuming two low-FODMAP vegetables together, it's a good idea to halve the permitted amounts to be on the safe side. If you have three, you have to "third" the amounts. It is possible that you, as an individual, can eat more than that, but it's better to be safe than sorry during the strict elimination stage of the diet.

WEIGHT LOSS AND WEIGHT GAIN

The low-FODMAP diet is not a weight loss or weight gain program. The amounts indicated on the plans are only for foods with a potential FODMAP issue. Other foods, such as protein-rich red meats, chicken, and fish, can be increased or decreased as appropriate so that the individual can maintain his or her weight.

The indicated amounts are the maximum amounts allowed. If you find that the indicated amount of a food is too much for you, then eat less of it, but don't cut out any one food group completely. Everyone is different, and it is up to you to find your personal balance. For instance, the caloric needs of a professional athlete will be different from those of a sedentary office worker who only exercises a couple of times a week.

HEADACHES

Headaches are common during the first week of the diet as your body detoxes from the wrong foods, especially caffeine and sugar. Even shifting from a diet comprised mostly of processed foods to a clean, whole-foods diet will help you detox from the added chemicals in manufactured foods. Don't worry: the headaches will soon disappear as your body adjusts.

SUPPLEMENTS

Stop taking all nonessential vitamin supplements (except vitamin D) so that you don't muddy the waters. Everything you put in your mouth can affect your gut. You can always test them later when you enter the reintroduction stage.

DELI MEATS

It's best to avoid deli meats because they are often marinated—perhaps with FODMAP-heavy garlic and onions. They may also contain preservatives that can increase your gut's hypersensitivity. Instead, eat fresh meats that you cook yourself.

CHEESE

Mature cheese is permitted because it is comprised mainly of fat and is therefore low in lactose. Fresh cheeses, such as mozzarella, cottage cheese, and ricotta, can be eaten in restricted amounts because some of the lactose leaks out into the liquid that is discarded during processing.

SUGAR

A certain amount of table sugar is okay on the diet because it has equal quantities of fructose and glucose. Exactly how much sugar you can tolerate is highly individual: the only way to find out is through trial and error. The glucose pulls the fructose, cell for cell, through the lining of the small intestine, so that it is absorbed.

If there is more fructose than glucose in a sweetener—as in most types of honeys and agave syrup, for instance—then the excess fructose will not be absorbed. Instead, it moves into the bowel where it is fermented, causing symptoms.

Still, if you're following a low-FODMAP diet, your consumption of "safe" sugars, such as table sugar or maple syrup, must be limited. That's because the glucose stops assisting with fructose absorption after awhile and the rest of the fructose moves down into the bowel. Again, the point at which this occurs is different in each person. That's why the meal plans include no added sugar, except in the form of a possible daily sweet treat. All other dietary sugar comes from your two daily servings of fruit.

MILK

You can either drink lactose-free dairy milk or an alternative such as rice, hemp, or almond milk. Dairy milk is preferable because it is much more nutritious. It has more protein and essential vitamins and minerals than nondairy alternatives, and it contains no sugar or undesirable additives, such as guar gum or xanthan gum, which may cause symptoms even though they are low-FODMAP. Always carefully check the ingredient lists on products.

YOGURT

Eat only lactose-free, sugar-free, fruit-free yogurt. Also, make sure that it doesn't contain inulin, which is high-FODMAP. If you prefer soy yogurt, be sure that it's made from the soy protein and not the whole bean. Coconut yogurt may be too rich, especially if it is made from coconut cream. If you've found that fat triggers your symptoms and you're watching your fat content accordingly, you should avoid it.

SALMON AND OTHER OILY FISH

Consuming oily fish is essential for good health because they contain high levels of omega-3 fatty acids. Their drawback is that they are high in fat, which is a gut irritant. Limit your intake to about 2 ounces (60 g) per serving.

BREAD

People following a low-FODMAP diet have no issue with gluten, which is a protein found in wheat, barley, and rye. Our issue is with the carbohydrates or fructans in those grains. Therefore, you cannot assume that gluten-free bread is also low-FODMAP. In fact, many gluten-free processed foods actually contain too much high-FODMAP almond meal, soy flour, or even coconut flour,

all of which can cause symptoms. Plus, any processed bread without gluten will contain several additives that help it hold together and taste good. These additives—such as guar gum, xanthan gum, and stabilizers—are potential problems, as are breads that contain too much fiber, because both may irritate the gut.

The safest option is to make your own low-FODMAP bread or choose a traditionally-made sourdough bread. In traditionally-made sourdough bread, which takes two days to make, no yeast is used: the wheat ferments, causing the dough to rise. Because fermentation has already occurred outside the body, it won't happen inside the body, so it's safe to eat.

Permitted flours include buckwheat flour, corn flour, maize flour, millet flour, quinoa flour, rice flour, sorghum flour, teff flour, tapioca flour, potato starch, and potato flour.

CRACKERS

As with bread, check the ingredients list and stick to the permitted flours and grains. Don't assume that a product is safe because it is gluten-free. Simple crackers with few ingredients are the best, such as rice crackers made only with rice and oil.

DRINKS

WATER

When you have IBS, water—which is FODMAP-free—is your main drink. In order to stay hydrated, you'll need to drink approximately eight 8-ounce (235 ml) glasses of water a day. You may need more water if you have a physically active lifestyle or live in a hot climate. To achieve this, have one glass of water with each meal and one in between each meal. Always sip your water slowly: don't drink it all at once.

JUICE

Be careful with juices. The fruits and vegetables from which they're made are concentrated in the juice and will almost certainly be above safe FODMAP levels. If you don't have reflux, you can have half a glass of orange juice, but eating the whole fruit is always preferable because it contains fiber. You can also have an 8-ounce (235 ml) glass of sugar-free, additive-free cranberry juice.

TEA AND COFFEE

Both tea and coffee contain caffeine, which is a gut irritant, but you can have up to one cup (8 ounces or 235 ml) of weak tea or coffee a day during the program. A good caffeine-free alternative is herbal tea, though many types are high in FODMAPs, such as chamomile and fennel teas, as well as fruit-based teas with chicory root. Peppermint tea and ginger tea may be safe, but watch out for any other ingredients—besides the herb itself, that is—that may have been added to processed products. You should avoid peppermint tea if you have reflux.

ALCOHOLIC BEVERAGES

As a gut irritant, alcohol is best avoided. It's up to you to decide whether or not you want to include it in your lifestyle and how often you want to consume it. That said, here are some guidelines on FODMAPs and alcoholic drinks.

WINE

From a FODMAP point of view, because wine is made from grapes, you can have one five-ounce (150 ml) glass of dry red or white wine at a meal. However, you should limit your intake and avoid it during the elimination stage.

HOW TO ADD FLAVOR TO FOOD

A low-FODMAP diet doesn't have to be boring. Here are some tips for adding zing to your meals:

- Dress your salad yourself with vinegar, lemon or lime juice, a little olive oil, salt, and pepper. Most ready-made dressings contain garlic, which is high in fructans.

- Use up to two tablespoons (30 ml) of Worcestershire sauce per meal. It may contain a little garlic, but it's in such a small amount that it won't be an issue.

- Use up to two tablespoons (30 ml) of soy sauce per meal.

- Add plain spices of your choice. Avoid spice mixes because they sometimes contain garlic, onions and/or wheat.

- Add your favorite herbs.

- Use garlic- and onion-infused oils. The FODMAPS in garlic and onions are not soluble in oil—even though they are soluble in liquids—so garlic- and onion-infused oils are suitable for a low-FODMAP diet. If you have reflux, don't consume more than one teaspoon at each meal. Also, don't make and store garlic and onion oils yourself because there is a risk of botulism: The bacteria spores that cause botulism can spread in certain foods when they're not exposed to oxygen, as is the case when you infuse garlic in oil.

SPIRITS

One ounce (30 ml) of spirits—apart from rum, which is high in fructose—per sitting is permitted from a FODMAP point of view. You should limit your intake because of the alcohol content. Also, be careful when you choose a mixer for your spirits: a sugary carbonated drink will irritate your gut.

BEER

From a FODMAP point of view, one twelve-ounce (360 ml) can of beer per sitting is permitted as long as it doesn't contain mannitol, which is high-FODMAP. Of course, it does contain both alcohol and carbonation, both of which are gut irritants, so you'll need to limit your intake.

STOCK

There are a few onion- and garlic-free stocks on the market, but they aren't widely available. If you can't find one, make your own stock with a chicken carcass, beef bones, or a fish skeleton, plus herbs, spices, and permitted vegetables (such as carrots, celery, and the green part of spring onions). Put them into a large saucepan, add enough water to cover all the ingredients, bring to a boil, and simmer for 3 to 4 hours to concentrate the flavor. Strain before using.

CREATING NEW HABITS

Over the coming six weeks, you will be breaking old habits and creating new, healthier ones. But

LABEL READING

When you buy packaged foods, always check the labels. Look for the following words and phrases because these ingredients could irritate your gut:

- Sweeteners, including high-fructose corn syrup (HFCS), agave, yacon syrup, honey, and anything with high fructose levels

- Artificial sweeteners, especially those ending in "-ol," such as mannitol or sorbitol

- Inulin and chicory root found in yogurt, breads, and crackers (They may appear as "dietary fiber" on ingredient labels.)

- Garlic and onions can be hidden behind the words "spices" or "natural flavors." (In the United States, the term "spices" is safe; it never includes either garlic or onions.)

- High-FODMAP dried fruits in cereals and snack bars

- Gums, such as guar gum and xanthan gum (Gluten-free processed foods contain these gums in place of the gluten. Such gums are low-FODMAP, but they ferment in the body and can be gut irritants.)

In general, it's best to stay away from processed foods. Instead, buy single-ingredient foods from the fresh sections of the supermarket.

it's important to not make too many changes at once or you'll feel overwhelmed. That's why you should focus on one lifestyle area at a time. You'll see that in this program, we'll treat a single area of a balanced lifestyle at a time: sleep in week 1, stress in week 2, and so on. That'll help you stick to your new habits. And, of course, you'll need willpower to stay the course until a new pathway in the brain has been formed and the new habit is established.

The most important habits for you to form are healthy dietary ones: specifically, the number and size of your meals. Eating your meals at the same time each day will help you settle into a routine. That way, you won't skip meals and then gorge yourself—consuming an overload of FODMAPs in the process.

STRATEGIES FOR STICKING TO YOUR NEW HABITS

- Make each of your lifestyle changes a priority. Schedule them into your day and repeat them until you're so used to them that you feel like something is wrong if you *don't* perform them.

- Be sure to write your lifestyle changes down. If you only keep a list in your head, you're sure to forget to do them—and you won't create new pathways in your brain that way.

- Keep track of your new activities in a notebook—or even on a whiteboard—and record when you do and don't perform them. That'll make you much more accountable for your actions.

- Get your family on board with your new habits and even include them in some, if possible. That way, you'll be accountable to each other.

- During this habit-forming period, don't focus on results: focus only on the activity itself. Results can take time—especially when it comes to exercise, for instance—and you don't want to give up because you're not seeing visible improvement quickly.

- Tying the new habit to an existing part of your daily routine has been scientifically proven to increase your chances of maintaining the habit. Can you imagine not cleaning your teeth before going to bed? No? That's because the association between bed and cleaning your teeth is a powerful pathway in your brain. So, tie exercising to getting home from work, for example. Head straight to your closet and change into your tracksuit to go for a walk, and soon you'll find yourself doing it automatically.

- Never miss performing your new habit for two straight days, or you'll be in danger of letting it slide completely. If you miss one day, declare a state of emergency and make sure you perform the activity the next day. Skipping your activity must register as something monumental. That's because you're at your most fragile when you miss a day, and you are much more likely to throw in the towel and say, "To heck with it." That's when the big guns have to come out!

- Examine why you missed your activity and try to eliminate the "why" so that the obstacle isn't recurring.

With willpower, you'll be able to make lifestyle changes that'll equip you with a whole new set of healthy habits. That way, you can move into the future knowing you'll be able to keep your IBS symptoms under control. Good luck!

PART 2

THE **LOW-FODMAP** DIET PROGRAM

| WEEK ONE | **The Introduction and Elimination Phase**
Setting the Foundation for Success |

Now that you're equipped with background information on IBS and the low-FODMAP diet, it's time to dive in and start your journey toward a joyful, symptom-free life. It'll take dedication and focus, but the payoff is enormous. In fact, it's life-changing. To get there, you'll have to shed all your preconceptions regarding the definition of healthy eating. Do you think healthy means huge salads and fruit- and vegetable-rich smoothies? If so, you'll need to think again because both will aggravate your symptoms. This diet is its own healthy: it has just enough vegetables and fruit to supply you with all the vitamins and minerals you need without causing the hideous bloating and gas you're so familiar with.

The following meal plans are well-balanced, cover all the food groups, and contain an absolute minimum of processed foods. Processed foods include too many additives—both chemical and natural—for our hypersensitive digestive systems to tolerate. This is a clean, nutritious diet, and these meal plans could be quite different from the way you're eating now.

Remember that your current diet is making you sick, so it's best for you to commit to these meal plans one hundred percent and follow them closely. If you stick faithfully to the plans, your IBS symptoms will disappear quickly. If you try to adapt the meal plans to the way you used to eat, it will take longer to get results.

At the end of the day, the speed of your transformation depends on your commitment to the diet. Getting through the first week will take some determination, but the sourcing and preparation of low-FODMAP foods and meals will get simpler with time.

IBS WITH DIARRHEA

As terrible as your diarrhea has been and as limited as it has made your life until now, this type of IBS is the easiest to resolve. When you follow the diet accurately and adjust your intake of other gut irritants, your symptoms will disappear—possibly in the first few days.

IBS WITH CONSTIPATION

If you have IBS with constipation, you'll need to address your constipation on top of implementing the low-FODMAP diet. The diet alone will not solve the problem. Here are a few areas that you need to focus on in order to form stools that pass effortlessly:

FIBER

As you know from chapter 1, fiber is essential for good bowel movements, but too much will cause symptoms. That's why you'll need to increase your fiber intake gradually. Add the following to your diet one day at a time until your bowel movements are regular and easy to pass:

- Add 1 tablespoon (0.4 ounces, or 11 g) chia seeds—soaked in water or lactose-free milk— to your breakfast. Start with no more than this amount because too much could cause issues.

- If you don't see results, continue to eat the chia seeds, but assess the grains in your diet. If you have been eating a lot of white rice, for example, switch to brown rice or quinoa for one meal per day and see if that helps. (Watch that this doesn't tip you over your fiber limit, though.)

- If your constipation is still being stubborn, add some high-fiber cereal, such as ¼ cup (1.4 ounces, or 20 g) (uncooked measurement) of oats, to your breakfast. Be aware that oats may be too high in fiber for you as an individual.

The vast majority of IBS sufferers with constipation will have solved their problem at this stage. If none of these steps have worked for you, magnesium may help. It's a mild laxative, and it is often low in people with IBS. Magnesium citrate is easily digested: Start with a low dose, about 100 milligrams, to avoid diarrhea. Increase the dose slowly until your bowels pass firm stools easily. Follow the instructions on the bottle for the maximum dosage. Check with your doctor before taking magnesium.

WATER

Make sure you drink enough fluid: this will help keep your stools soft. When you have constipation, too much liquid is absorbed because of the slow movement of stools through the colon, so you need to make sure you don't aggravate the situation by not drinking enough water. Drink about eight glasses of water a day. (Caffeinated drinks and alcohol don't count: they're dehydrating.)

EXERCISE

It's important that you get plenty of exercise. If you have a sedentary job, get up and go for a walk around the office every now and then—or simply swing your arms around while sitting in your chair. The body loves big movements like these but it doesn't like the very small movements you make when you're working at a computer at all. Exercise helps the digestive system move the material through it and can help prevent constipation in this way.

Certain medications—including some antidepressants—can aggravate your constipation. Be sure to discuss this with your doctor.

MIXED IBS

If you have mixed IBS—that is, if you sometimes have diarrhea and sometimes have constipation— you'll probably find that your diarrhea will disappear on this diet, and you'll be left only with the constipation. If that happens, then follow the advice on constipation on this page.

Breakfast	CHEESE, CHICKEN, AND ZUCCHINI MUFFINS (page 32) *or* 4 ounces (125 g) chicken, ½ cup (60 g) zucchini, and 1 cup (138 g) potato *plus* ¼ cup (37 g) blueberries *and* weak tea or coffee (optional)
Morning Snack	PARMESAN AND SPINACH BALLS (page 36) *or* ¼ cup (55 g) cottage cheese, up to 20 small rice crackers, and 1 cup (30 g) spinach *and* 1 cup (235 ml) lactose-free milk
Lunch	1 or 2 lamb chops, 1 carrot, and 1 cup (185 g) cooked quinoa *plus* one just-ripe banana *and* a glass of water
Afternoon Snack	1 CRANBERRY AND WHITE CHOCOLATE OAT COOKIE (page 41), ¾ cup (170 g) lactose-free yogurt, ½ cup (70 g) sliced cucumber *or* up to 20 small rice crackers, ¾ cup (170 g) lactose-free yogurt, and ½ cup (70 g) sliced cucumber *and* a glass of water
Dinner	LEMON AND PARSLEY-CRUSTED SALMON WITH SPICY RICE AND BROCCOLI (page 49) *or* 1 salmon filet (about 2 ounces, or 60 g), 1 cup (70 g) broccoli florets, and 1 cup (165 g) cooked rice *and* a glass of water

Notes:

- While recipes have been suggested for the meal plans, feel free to choose an alternative from this week's recipes.
- The vegetables can be consumed either raw or cooked, but all measurements of vegetables in the meal plan are the uncooked measurements.
- If you can't find any lactose-free yogurt, have an extra glass of lactose-free milk to make sure your daily calcium needs are covered.
- If you find a full glass of milk is too much in one meal, have half a glass at two meals.
- Choose plain rice crackers which are made from as few ingredients as possible. Alternatively, you could have 2 rice cakes.

CHEESE, CHICKEN, AND ZUCCHINI MUFFINS

MAKES 22 MUFFINS (2 MUFFINS PER SERVING)

Make a batch of these savory muffins and freeze them. Then, just defrost them in the microwave for a quick, nutritious breakfast—or a complete snack—that includes all of the food groups.

8.8 ounces (250 g) cooked mashed potato

1 cup (235 ml) water

¼ cup (60 ml) light olive oil

2 eggs, lightly beaten

½ cup (79 g) white rice flour

¼ cup (32 g) tapioca flour

¼ cup (48 g) potato starch

2 teaspoons (9 g) baking powder

½ teaspoon salt

1 teaspoon ground turmeric

¼ teaspoon ground black pepper

1 zucchini, finely chopped

4.4 ounces (125 g) Camembert, diced

3.5 ounces (100 g) cooked chicken, chopped

Preheat the oven to 350°F (180°C, or gas mark 4). Grease two 12-cup muffin pans with oil. Combine the mashed potato, water, oil, and eggs. Sift the dry ingredients together and then gently fold the wet ingredients into the dry. Stir in the zucchini, cheese, and chicken and combine (but do not overmix). Spoon the batter into the muffin pans, filling each cup full. Bake for about 20 minutes or until a toothpick inserted into the center of a muffin comes out clean. Let the muffins cool on a wire rack before serving. Store leftovers in the fridge for 3 days or freeze for up to 3 months.

FISH OMELET

SERVES 4

Omelets make quick, easy breakfasts—or lunches or dinners. The fish could be replaced with any other protein meat, such as chicken, while the potato could be leftover sweet potato (½ cup [55 g] per omelet), and even the bok choy could be an equal quantity of spinach or kale.

1 tablespoon (15 ml) light olive oil

1 red chile, deseeded and finely chopped (omit for reflux)

2 spring onions, chopped (green parts only)

3 filets of firm white fish, such as cod or haddock, chopped

3 medium cooked potatoes, sliced

8 eggs

½ cup (117 ml) lactose-free milk

Salt and pepper

3 cups (210 g) chopped bok choy

1 tablespoon (1 g) roughly chopped cilantro

1 tablespoon (5 g) grated Parmesan cheese

Preheat the broiler. Heat the oil an ovenproof skillet and add the chile (if using) and spring onions. Cook for 1 minute. Add the fish and potatoes and cook until the potatoes are lightly browned.

Beat the eggs, milk, salt, and pepper in a large bowl and add the bok choy. When the fish is almost cooked through, add the egg mixture to the skillet. Cook until the base of the omelet is set, about 5 to 8 minutes. Sprinkle with the cilantro and Parmesan. Place under the broiler until the top of the omelet is set, about 5 minutes. Serve immediately. Store leftovers in the fridge for 1 day.

BANANA PANCAKES WITH CINNAMON RICOTTA AND KIWI

SERVES 4

These thick, tasty pancakes are delicious topped with any low-FODMAP fruit. Just be sure to adjust the amount of fruit you use so that you don't consume more than 1 serving of fruit per meal because banana is already in the pancake batter. You can also replace the ricotta with up to 4 tablespoons (55 g) of cottage cheese or ½ cup (30 g) of whipped cream per serving. Make it a complete meal by pairing it with a vegetable, such as 1 carrot, 5 snow peas, or 1 cup (72 g) of lettuce.

2 just-ripe bananas, mashed

4 eggs

1 teaspoon vanilla extract

Butter, for cooking

8 tablespoons (125 g) ricotta

½ teaspoon ground cinnamon

2 kiwis, peeled and sliced

Maple syrup

Beat the bananas, eggs, and vanilla together until well blended.

Melt a little butter in a skillet. Once it is bubbling, pour a quarter of the pancake mixture into the skillet. Cook until set on one side, about 3 to 5 minutes, and then flip it over and cook until set on the other side. Slide the pancake onto a plate and keep warm. Cook the rest of the pancake mixture in the same way.

Combine the ricotta with the cinnamon. Top each pancake with a quarter of the sliced kiwi and 2 tablespoons (about 30 g) of the ricotta mixture. Drizzle with a little maple syrup and serve immediately. Store leftover pancakes (without toppings) in the fridge for 3 to 4 days or freeze for 2 to 3 months.

PARMESAN AND SPINACH BALLS

SERVES 4

This vegetarian recipe calls for just a handful of simple ingredients. These spinach balls cover all the necessary food groups, and they're perfect as a complete morning or afternoon snack or as nibbles to serve guests when they drop around for drinks. For a little variety, make them with kale instead of spinach and replace the Parmesan with any mature cheese. Serve them with a garlic- and onion-free mayonnaise, if you like.

4.2 ounces (120 g) spinach

2 eggs

¾ cup (75 g) Parmesan cheese, grated

1 cup (115 g) gluten-free day-old breadcrumbs

1 tablespoon (3 g) finely chopped fresh thyme

½ teaspoon paprika

Salt and pepper

Preheat the oven to 350°F (180°C, or gas mark 4). Place the spinach in a food processor and pulse until very finely chopped. Add all the other ingredients to the food processor and pulse again until well combined.

Form the spinach mixture into balls and place on a baking sheet lined with parchment paper. Place in the oven and bake for 20 to 25 minutes. Serve immediately or let cool, refrigerate, and eat cold. Store in the fridge for 3 to 4 days or freeze for 2 to 3 months.

TOMATO, LEEK, AND TURKEY BRUSCHETTA

SERVES 4 (1 SLICE PER SERVING)

Classic Italian bruschetta is wonderful as an appetizer: Cut each bruschetta into four pieces to create delicious nibbles to serve at a party or with drinks. Vary the toppings however you like (as long as you stick to low-FODMAP foods). To stay within the FODMAP limits for your meal, have no more than one slice.

4 slices of low-FODMAP bread

3 tablespoons (45 ml) light olive oil, divided

2 tomatoes, diced (omit for reflux)

4 tablespoons (24 g) chopped leeks
    (green parts only)

2 teaspoons (10 ml) garlic-infused oil
    (omit for reflux)

Salt and pepper

Sliced cooked turkey,
    enough to cover the bread

2 tablespoons (10 g) grated Parmesan
    cheese (½ tablespoon per slice), to serve

Preheat the broiler. Place the bread on a baking sheet and place under the broiler until toasted on one side, about 3 to 5 minutes.

Meanwhile, heat 1 tablespoon (15 ml) of the olive oil in a skillet. Add the tomatoes (if using) and leeks. Cook until the leeks are softened, about 3 to 5 minutes. Season with salt and pepper.

When the bread is toasted on one side, remove from the oven and drizzle the untoasted side with the remaining olive oil and the garlic oil (if using). Top with the sliced turkey and then the leek mixture and the Parmesan. Place the bruschetta under the broiler again until the cheese is melted. Season to taste and serve immediately.

FETA AND TUNA DIP

SERVES 4

This rich, nourishing dip is a great snack-time partner for gluten-free crackers and vegetable sticks. Have a quarter of this dip with rice crackers and a vegetable, such as ½ cup (60 g) zucchini, ½ cup (70 g) cucumber, or 2 radishes. It's ideal for sharing, so offer it to guests with drinks, or bring it along as your contribution to a shared meal.

7 ounces (200 g) feta cheese,
   broken into pieces
3.2 ounces (90 g) canned tuna
   in spring water, drained
½ teaspoon wasabi
½ celery stalk, roughly chopped
1 tablespoon (3 g) chives,
   roughly chopped
2 tablespoons (15 g) walnuts

Place the feta in a food processor. Add the tuna and wasabi and blend well until the mixture becomes a smooth paste. Add the celery, chives, and walnuts and pulse again to combine (but do not overblend). Place the dip in the fridge for 2 hours before serving. Store in the fridge for 2 to 3 days.

RASPBERRY CUSTARD CAKE

MAKES 12 SLICES

This moist, creamy cake presents beautifully, so it's sure to impress guests at your next dinner party. Vary the fruit if you want, but the kiwi slices look great when they're arranged in a border around the cake's edge. If the top of the cake looks like it may burn partway through baking, cover it with aluminum foil and then return it to the oven.

For the pastry

8.8 ounces (250 g) butter

1 cup (200 g) sugar

1 teaspoon vanilla extract

2 teaspoons (10 ml) lemon juice

4 egg yolks

2 cups (316 g) white rice flour

½ cup (64 g) tapioca flour

½ cup (96 g) potato starch

For the custard

3 eggs

2 tablespoons (16 g) corn flour

8.8 ounces (250 g) plain lactose-free yogurt

½ cup (100 g) sugar

1 teaspoon vanilla extract

To assemble

2 kiwis, peeled and thinly sliced

2 cups (250 g) raspberries

First, prepare the pastry. Preheat the oven to 350°F (180°C, or gas mark 4). Cream together the butter and sugar until light and fluffy. Mix in the vanilla and lemon juice. Beat the egg yolks in one at a time until well incorporated. Sift the flours together and then add them to the wet ingredients and mix gently until just combined. Butter and line a 9-inch (23 cm) springform cake pan. Halve the pastry dough and press one half into the base of the pan.

To prepare the custard, whisk together all the ingredients until well blended.

To assemble the cake, arrange the kiwi slices along the inside upright edge of the cake pan. Spread the raspberries over the pastry base and pour the custard over the top. Crumble up the remaining pastry and arrange the crumbles over the top of the custard. Bake for 20 to 25 minutes until the pastry is browned and the custard is set. Remove from the oven and let cool in the pan for 10 minutes.

Gently release the springform and lift it away from the cake. Slip a wide spatula underneath the cake and transfer it to a serving plate. Let cool completely before slicing and serving. Store in the fridge for 3 to 4 days—although you're sure to eat it all before then!

CRANBERRY AND WHITE CHOCOLATE OAT COOKIES

MAKES 16 COOKIES

Have just one of these cookies after they come out of the oven and freeze the rest of them to keep them fresh (and out of temptation's way)—then either eat another straight from the freezer or defrost in the microwave when snack time rolls around again. Don't worry about the amount of dairy in the chocolate chips; it's negligible when divided among 16 cookies, so unless you're intolerant to the casein in dairy, these will be fine.

3.2 ounces (90 g) butter

¾ cup (195 g) peanut butter

2 eggs

¾ cup (150 g) white sugar

1 teaspoon vanilla extract

¼ cup (48 g) potato starch

¼ cup (32 g) tapioca flour

¼ cup (40 g) white rice flour

1 teaspoon baking soda

Pinch of salt

1½ cups (120 g) dried oats
    (use the fine ones)

¾ cup (90 g) dried cranberries

1 cup (175 g) white chocolate chips

Preheat the oven to 350°F (180°C, or gas mark 4). Place the butter, peanut butter, eggs, sugar, and vanilla in a food processor and process until well mixed.

Sift the potato starch, flours, baking soda, and salt together in a bowl. Add the oats, cranberries, and chocolate chips and mix well. Fold the wet ingredients into the dry and combine. Drop the cookie dough in spoonfuls on a baking sheet lined with parchment paper. Mold each into a cookie shape. (They will spread a little during baking.) Bake for about 6 minutes and then cool on a wire rack. Eat fresh or cool completely, transfer to an airtight container, and freeze for up 2 to 3 months.

CHOCOLATE AND ORANGE POLENTA CAKE

MAKES 12 SLICES

This moist, easy-to-make chocolate-orange cake is perfect with a cup of tea or coffee. If you feel that fructose is one of your biggest symptom-triggers, leave out the orange syrup; it'll still be delicious. Be sure to stick to one slice per serving.

For the cake

5.3 ounces (150 g) butter,
    at room temperature
5.3 ounces (150 g) superfine granulated
    white sugar
3 eggs
1½ (8 g) tablespoons cocoa powder
1½ tablespoons (25 ml) hot water
⅓ cup (32 g) ground almonds
½ teaspoon baking powder
1 teaspoon ground cinnamon
⅓ cup (47 g) quick-cook fine-grain polenta
1 tablespoon (6 g) grated orange peel
½ cup (55 g) chopped pecans
12 whole pecans

For the syrup

Juice of 1 orange
1.8 ounces (50 g) granulated sugar

For the glaze

1 cup (120 g) powdered sugar
1 to 2 tablespoons (15 to 30 ml)
    orange juice
Water (if needed)

First, make the cake. Preheat the oven to 325°F (170°C, or gas mark 3). Grease a 7.5-in (19 cm) springform cake pan and line with parchment paper. Beat the butter and sugar together until pale and fluffy, about 5 minutes. Beat in the eggs, one at a time. Mix the cocoa with the hot water and stir until dissolved. Then fold into the butter mixture.

In a separate bowl, combine the almonds, baking powder, cinnamon, polenta, and orange peel. Add the wet ingredients to the dry ingredients and stir in the pecans. Spoon the mixture into the cake pan and bake on the middle shelf of the oven for about 35 minutes or until a toothpick inserted into the center comes out clean. Allow to cool slightly in the pan.

Then, prepare the syrup. Combine the orange juice with the sugar in a small saucepan. Bring to the boil and simmer, stirring regularly, for 5 minutes or until slightly reduced and thickened. Make holes in the cake with a skewer and pour syrup over the cake while it is still hot. When cool, remove the cake from the pan.

Finally, prepare the glaze. Mix the powdered sugar and orange juice to form a thin paste. Add water if necessary to reach a runny, pourable consistency. Pour the glaze over the cooled cake and let it drip over the edges. Garnish each slice with a whole pecan. Allow the glaze to set and then serve. Store in an airtight container for 2 days or freeze in slices for 2 to 3 months.

CHICKEN AND WALNUT COLESLAW

SERVES 4

Simple, filling, and delicious, this salad is a handy way to use up leftover cooked chicken. (There'll be plenty of leftovers for tomorrow's lunch, too.) It covers all the food groups. It also makes a great contribution to a shared meal: that way, there's sure to be at least one dish you can eat. Have around 1½ cups (175 g) to stay within the permitted FODMAP allowance for the meal.

4 medium new potatoes

1 carrot

¼ head of green cabbage

2 spring onions, roughly chopped
(green parts only)

¾ cup (90 g) walnut pieces, toasted

2 cups (280 g) chopped cooked chicken

1 cup (16 g) chopped cilantro, divided

1 teaspoon mustard

2 tablespoons (28 g) garlic- and
onion-free mayonnaise

1 tablespoon (15 ml) light olive oil

Salt and pepper

Chop the potatoes into bite-sized chunks and boil in salted water until just cooked. Drain and rinse with cold water a few times to cool. Set aside.

Meanwhile, peel the carrot and cut into large chunks. Chop the cabbage into 3 to 4 pieces. Place the carrot, cabbage, and spring onions in a food processor and pulse to chop (but take care not to chop them too finely). Alternatively, chop the vegetables by hand. Place in a serving bowl. Add the walnuts, chicken, half of the cilantro, and potatoes to the salad. Mix well.

Combine the mustard, mayonnaise, and oil in a small bowl. Add to the salad and mix gently until all the ingredients are well-coated. Adjust the seasoning to taste. Garnish with the remaining cilantro and serve. Store leftovers in the fridge for up to 3 days.

LAMB STIR-FRY

SERVES 4

If you're looking for a quick dinner that still uses fresh ingredients, try this flavorful lamb stir-fry. It's an excellent way to use up leftover vegetables, so feel free to change them up (the same goes for the meat, too). It's safe to eat up to a quarter of this recipe, but if you have a low tolerance for fat, use as little oil as possible. If you have reflux, omit the chile and bell pepper.

1 tablespoon (15 ml) light olive oil

½ cup (48 g) chopped leeks (green parts only)

1 green or red chile, chopped finely (omit for reflux)

2 teaspoons (4 g) grated gingerroot

14 ounces (400 g) ground lamb

1 red bell pepper, chopped (omit for reflux)

2 cups (180 g) chopped cabbage

1 zucchini, sliced, slices cut into quarters

1 tablespoon (15 ml) soy sauce

2 teaspoons (10 ml) fish sauce

Salt and pepper

Heat the oil in a skillet and then add the leeks, chile (if using), and ginger. Cook for 1 minute. Add the lamb and cook until almost browned through. Add all the vegetables and cook until softened but still crisp, about 5 to 8 minutes. Add the soy and fish sauces and adjust the seasoning. Serve hot with boiled or steamed rice. Store leftovers in the fridge for 2 to 3 days or freeze for 3 to 4 months.

PESTO PASTA

SERVES 4

It takes just six ingredients to pull together this complete vegetarian meal featuring all of the food groups. (If you have reflux, you may need to leave out the garlic-infused oil.) You can use any type of low-FODMAP pasta you like with pesto, but spaghetti or tagliatelle are the traditional choices. If you have a low tolerance for fat, this may not be the best choice for you because the quantity of oil may trigger your symptoms.

WEEK ONE
Dinners

17.6 ounces (500 g) low-FODMAP spaghetti

2 cups (48 g) fresh basil leaves

3.9 ounces (110 g) Parmesan cheese, plus more for serving

2 tablespoons (18 g) pine nuts

2 teaspoons (10 ml) garlic-infused oil (omit for reflux)

3.4 ounces (100 ml) olive oil

Salt and pepper

Fill a large saucepan with plenty of water and bring to the boil. Add 1 tablespoon (9 g) of salt. When the water has reached a rolling boil, add the spaghetti. Stir while the water returns to the boil. Cook until al dente.

Meanwhile, place the basil, Parmesan, and pine nuts in a small food processor and process well. Add the garlic oil (if using) and olive oil and process again. Season to taste.

Drain the cooked pasta and place in a large bowl. Add the pesto sauce and mix well. Serve immediately, with fresh Parmesan grated over the top. Store leftovers in the fridge for 3 days.

TUNA MOUSSE

SERVES 4

Tuna mousse is ideal for a simple dinner or lunch, and it's such a pretty dish to serve to guests. (Feel free to replace the tuna with canned salmon if you like.) Enjoy it with 1 cup (72 g) of mixed salad and some sourdough bread or a serving of potato salad.

10.6 ounces (300 g) canned tuna, drained

2 tablespoons (28 g) garlic- and onion-free mayonnaise

2 tablespoons (28 g) plain lactose-free yogurt

½ teaspoon salt

Ground black pepper

4 drops of Tabasco

Lemon zest

½ lemon

0.5 ounces (14 g) gelatin

3 tablespoons (45 ml) water

2 pasteurized egg whites

Add the tuna to a food processor with the mayonnaise, yogurt, salt, pepper, and Tabasco. Grate the zest of the halved lemon into the mixture and then squeeze in its juice.

Dissolve the gelatin in the water in a small saucepan placed over a gentle heat. Add the mixture to the processor and pulse well. Whip the egg whites until stiff and then fold them into the tuna mixture.

Lightly oil four 3-inch (8 cm) molds. Spoon a quarter of the mixture into each and place in the fridge to set for at least 2 hours. Once set, unmold and serve cold. Store in the fridge for 2 to 3 days.

LEMON AND PARSLEY-CRUSTED SALMON WITH SPICY RICE AND BROCCOLI

SERVES 4

Packed with omega-3 fatty acids, salmon is a high-quality protein. It's an oily fish, though, and you may want to go easy on it. Fat can trigger your symptoms because it's a gut irritant. Stick to one—or maybe two—servings per week.

For the salmon

2 fresh salmon filets
(4 x 4 in [10 x 10 cm] each)
2 tablespoons (30 ml) melted butter
1 slice of low-FODMAP bread
1 spring onion (green part only)
1 tablespoon (6 g) grated lemon peel
1 tablespoon (4 g) chopped fresh parsley
Salt and pepper

For the rice

1½ cups (270 g) uncooked jasmine rice
4 cups (280 g) broccoli florets
4 teaspoons (20 g) Dijon mustard
3 teaspoons (15 ml) soy sauce
4 drops of Tabasco

Preheat the oven to 350°F (180°C, or gas mark 4). Lightly oil a shallow baking sheet. Pat the salmon dry with a paper towel. Place the salmon, skin-side down, in the oiled baking sheet and brush with 1 tablespoon (15 ml) of the butter. Sprinkle with salt.

Place the bread, spring onion, lemon peel, and parsley in a small food processor and pulse. Pour in the remaining butter and pulse again until the mixture forms breadcrumbs. Press the breadcrumb mixture evenly on top of the salmon. Bake uncovered for 15 to 25 minutes or until the salmon flakes easily with a fork. (Cooking time depends on the thickness of fish filet: Don't overcook it, or it will become dry.)

To make the spicy rice and broccoli, cook the rice according to the package instructions. Boil the broccoli in a saucepan of boiling water, about 4 to 5 minutes, or steam it. Combine the mustard, soy sauce, and Tabasco and add it to the cooked rice. Gently stir the broccoli into the rice and adjust the seasoning to taste. Serve the salmon with the rice.

STEAK AND MASHED POTATO
WITH CHIMICHURRI SAUCE

SERVES 4

This is comfort food at its best—and the flavorful chimichurri topping lifts this simple dish to another level. Have no more than a quarter of the potatoes, one steak, and about 3 tablespoons (45 g) of the sauce to stay low-FODMAP. (If you have reflux, use less chile or omit it altogether.) Reserve the white ends of the bok choy for a low-FODMAP soup, such as the Leftover Soup on page 176.

WEEK ONE
Dinners

For the steak

4 sirloin steaks (1 inch [2.5 cm] thick)

Salt and pepper

For the mashed potatoes

4 white potatoes (about 4 ounces or
     120 g each), peeled

1.7 ounces (50 g) butter

2 tablespoons (30 ml) lactose-free milk

Salt and pepper

For the chimichurri sauce

2 bunches of bok choy, leaves separated
     and washed well (green parts only)

1 small bunch of fresh parsley

1 red chile (omit for reflux)

1 spring onion (green part only)

1 teaspoon sugar

Juice from ½ a lemon

1 teaspoon garlic-infused oil
     (omit for reflux)

2 tablespoons (30 ml) olive oil

Salt and pepper

First, prepare the steaks. Place them on a hot grill and cook for about 2 minutes on each side for medium rare. (Exact cooking time depends on the thickness of the steak.) Season with salt and pepper. Let the steaks sit for 10 minutes under aluminum foil and then slice them against the grain.

Make the mashed potatoes. Chop the potatoes roughly and boil in salted water until soft. Drain well and then add the butter and milk. Season to taste and mash until creamy.

To make the chimichurri sauce, place the bok choy leaves in a food processor with the parsley, chile (if using), and spring onion. Process until very fine. Add the sugar, lemon juice, garlic oil (if using), and olive oil. Process again and add more oil if necessary. Add 1 tablespoon (14 g) of the mashed potatoes to make the sauce creamy. Mix well and then season to taste.

To serve, divide the mashed potatoes between four plates and layer the sliced steak over each. Top each with 1 tablespoon (15 g) of the chimichurri sauce and place the rest in a serving bowl for the table. Store leftover meat and sauce separately in the fridge for 2 to 3 days.

CHICKEN CACCIATORE

SERVES 4

This fragrant, warming dish is especially satisfying during the winter months. Serve it with a grain, such as rice or quinoa, to help soak up the sauce and make it a complete meal. If you have leftover sauce, serve it the next day for lunch over low-FODMAP pasta, plus any chicken and low-FODMAP vegetables that might be lingering in the fridge. This recipe is not suitable if you have reflux.

1 tablespoon (15 ml) light olive oil

4 chicken legs and thighs

2 spring onions, sliced (green parts only)

¼ cup (64 g) tomato paste

¾ cup (175 ml) white wine

¾ cup (175 ml) garlic- and onion-free chicken broth

½ teaspoon oregano

½ teaspoon basil

1 bay leaf

2 tomatoes, chopped

1 large green pepper, chopped

Heat the olive oil in a large skillet. Add the chicken and brown on all sides, about 5 minutes per side. Add the spring onions and cook for 1 minute. Add all the ingredients, except the tomatoes and green pepper, and mix well so that the chicken is covered in the sauce. Cover and simmer for 35 minutes. Add the vegetables and cook, covered, for another 20 minutes. Remove the bay leaf. Serve immediately. Store leftovers in the fridge for 2 to 3 days or freeze for 2 to 3 months.

DIARY PAGE | **WEEK ONE** | DATE ___/___/___

SLEEP _____ hours   from _____ to _____

Quality of sleep _____

_____

_____

_____

BOWEL MOVEMENTS _____ number   times _____

Type* _____

_____

_____

_____

MEDICATION

Type _____

_____

_____

_____

SUPPLEMENTS

Type _____   _____

_____   _____

_____   _____

_____   _____

*To find what type of bowel movement you've had, search the Internet for "Bristol Stool Chart."

FOOD JOURNAL | WEEK ONE

MEAL	TIME	NOTES/SYMPTOMS
Breakfast		
Morning snack		
Lunch		
Afternoon snack		
Dinner		

Lifestyle Exercise: **SLEEP**

The Centers for Disease Control and Prevention (CDC) have called sleep deprivation a public health crisis. According to a recent CDC study, more than a third of American adults are not getting enough sleep on a regular basis. This has significant implications for people with IBS: According to Jonathan Cedernaes, a sleep researcher at Uppsala University in Sweden, a new research study has demonstrated a link between lack of sleep and a change in gut bacteria.

WHAT SLEEP DOES FOR YOU

- While you are sleeping, your brain is preparing you for the next day by clearing unused pathways and forming new ones to help you learn and remember information.

- Sleep helps you pay attention and stay focused, and it improves your decision-making skills.

- Sleep helps you control your emotions and behavior, and it helps you cope with change.

- Sleep is involved in the healing and repair of your heart and blood vessels.

- Sleep deficiency increases the risk of obesity because sleep helps maintain a healthy balance of the hormones that make you feel hungry (ghrelin) or full (leptin).

- Sleep deficiency results in a higher-than-normal blood sugar level, which may increase your risk for diabetes.

- Sleep helps build your immune system so your body can fight common infections.

HOW MUCH SLEEP DO YOU NEED?

In general, most healthy adults are built for 16 hours of wakefulness, which means they need an average of eight hours of sleep a night.

CAUSES OF SLEEPING DIFFICULTIES

Apart from rarer physiological and psychological disorders that may be involved, the following things can cause sleeping difficulties:

- Stress: for example, job-related pressures or a family problem

- Drinking beverages containing alcohol or caffeine in the afternoon or evening

- Exercising close to bedtime

- Following an irregular morning and nighttime schedule

- Working or studying right before getting into bed

- Environmental factors, such as a room that's too hot or cold, too noisy, or too brightly lit.

- Interruptions from children or other family members

- Physical problems that cause pain

- Medications such as decongestants, steroids, and some medicines for high blood pressure, asthma, or depression

Your Exercise This Week:
8 HOURS OF SLEEP A NIGHT

Let's suppose you go to bed at 10 p.m. and get up at 6 a.m. Here's how to maximize your chances of a good night's sleep:

- No caffeine after 6 p.m.

- No food or alcohol after 7 p.m.

- At 9 p.m., stop all heavy mental activity and relax (preferably without using electronic devices).

- At 9 p.m., stop drinking water.

- Minimize noise, light, and excessive hot or cold temperatures in your bedroom.

- Don't engage in any non-sleep activities in the bedroom, such as reading or watching TV.

Diet Integration:
BARRIERS TO SUCCESS

THE LITTLE DEVIL ON YOUR SHOULDER

We all have that little devil that sit on one of our shoulders, trying to derail our good intentions at every turn. Plus, we may have been indoctrinated with subtle negative messages over time, and this can cause feelings of guilt and shame that work to undermine our self-confidence and self-esteem.

If you are struggling to stick to the diet with little success, some of the following factors might be affecting you.

Stress

Many people react to stress by heading straight for food—and not just any food, but fatty or sweet foods, which do the most damage. Too much fat is a gut irritant, and too many sweet foods can result in a fructose overload.

Sometimes, an emotional upset makes you reach for comfort food, and that's okay: Just make sure it is still low-FODMAP. There are several recipes for sweet treats in this book, so make sure you have some on hand for when stress kicks in. Avoiding stress completely isn't always possible, so when it hits, be sure to employ the deep breathing relaxation technique you will learn in week 2 on page 87.

Depression

As mentioned in chapter 1, there is a link between IBS and depression, which may be caused by your body's inability to properly absorb the nutrients in your food. Now that you're on the low-FODMAP diet, you should notice that your mood has started to improve.

Cost

Whether you follow a "normal" diet or a more restricted one, food costs money and there's a popular misconception that special diets are expensive. But this isn't so. Indian and other Asian shops can be good places to buy cheap low-FODMAP supplies, especially low-FODMAP flours, such as rice flour, potato starch, and tapioca flour. Always buy your fruit and vegetables in season so that they are fresh and inexpensive and keep frozen fruit and vegetables on hand as backups.

Time Constraints

Many people will tell you they don't have enough time to cook complete meals or to bake: instead, they purchase processed foods as shortcuts. The time you spend on cooking will reward you with good health because the chemicals in most processed foods are harmful for those with IBS. Cooking at home doesn't have to be difficult. Steaming vegetables and a piece of fish couldn't be simpler. You can save time by batch-cooking and freezing meals, too.

Instead of spending mindless time in front of electronic devices, head to the kitchen and use your time wisely by preparing your own meals. We like to claim that we "have no time" these days, but the truth is that we do. We just need to make better choices about how we spend it.

Temptation

Temptations are everywhere. For instance, you're out and about in the car and you're starving when you pass a fast-food joint. Or you're out with friends at a cocktail party and everyone is grabbing the delicious nibbles that are passed around. Maybe your mother has come to visit and has brought luscious cream cakes with her. Eliminating temptation is an almost impossible feat. You'll have to be strong and well-prepared with tactics to divert your attention from the temptation.

To avoid the lure of fast food, make sure you carry snacks in your bag so you never get desperately hungry. Eat before going to cocktail parties so you're not tempted to eat once you're there. Pull some low-FODMAP muffins out of the freezer and microwave them if your mother turns up with forbidden food. (Let her have the cream cakes.)

TIPS FOR BREAKING DOWN THESE BARRIERS

- Try to understand why and how things went wrong—so wrong that you made a choice that wasn't consistent with reaching your goals. If you can get to the bottom of the circumstances surrounding your slipup, you'll be able to eliminate that barrier the next time. For example, if you got takeout from that fast-food place you saw when you were starving, now you know that you need to take food with you the next time you're out so that you don't let yourself get that hungry. Problem solved!

- Be compassionate with yourself when you err. Would you be this harsh on a friend if he or she made the same mistake? No. So treat yourself in the same way that you would treat someone else. Don't beat yourself up.

- In the same way, be encouraging to yourself, just as you would with a friend. Talk to yourself about how wonderfully you are doing overall and try to get past what happened. You need encouragement, just like everyone else.

When you transgress, it is important that you are kind to yourself. It is also very, very important that you strengthen your resolve and learn from your mistake so that you never do it again. Changing from a lifetime of blame, guilt, and shame to one that's compassionate and understanding is a big step. If you acknowledge the process, you've already made a big step in the right direction.

ROSLYN

Roslyn came to me in desperation because her IBS symptoms of diarrhea, bloating, and pain had become unbearable. When I asked her why she thought they had escalated to this level, she explained that Geoff, her beloved husband of forty-five years, had recently been diagnosed with Alzheimer's disease. They had just moved into a retirement village and were frantically trying to sell their condominium: if they couldn't, they would shortly run out of money. She was only getting four to five hours of sleep a night because the full responsibility of their situation was on her shoulders: Geoff was no longer able to make decisions.

Despite her burden, Roslyn had enough awareness to know that she had to address her health before she could move forward. She began the low-FODMAP diet on the following Monday. Her symptoms quickly abated due to her dedication to the process. She followed the diet closely, and forgave herself when she slipped up once or twice.

Plus, she created a routine in which she and Geoff were in bed at the same time each night and got up eight hours later. And she incorporated a special sleep game I use myself into that routine. When it comes to sleep, the key is to focus your mind on something other than your own random thoughts.

Our minds are powerful, independent creatures, but we can control them with effort, consistency, and determination. When I wake and can't get back to sleep, I pick a specific topic to focus on, such as countries of the world or girls' names—anything that comprises a list. Then, I work my way through the alphabet and (silently) say one country for each letter: Austria, Botswana, Canada, Denmark, and so on. (If your list has many possibilities, you could come up with two "entries" for each letter.) When you get stuck and can't think of one, continue to try for a bit—but then move on. The idea is to engross the mind so that those unwanted thoughts don't dominate you. After you have done this consistently for several nights, your body will quickly get the signal that it's about to go to sleep. (I seldom get past "D" these days.) It's about creating new pathways in the brain with associations: In this case, the association is "letter game equals sleep." Soon, Roslyn was recording six, seven, and eventually eight hours of uninterrupted sleep each night.

Roslyn had an enormous incentive to resolve her health issues, and she succeeded spectacularly. In fact, after the six-week program, she decided she was well enough that she and Geoff could move back to their condominium and leave retirement-village living for the time being.

WEEK TWO

Relief
Becoming Symptom-Free

If you've been diligently following the meal plans in chapter 1, have gotten your timing right when it comes to meals, and have established a regular sleep pattern, you're probably feeling a great deal of relief already. If you have IBS with diarrhea, your symptoms will have disappeared. If you have IBS with constipation, your bloating and excess gas should be a thing of the past, but you may still be adjusting your fiber levels in order to relieve your constipation.

If the diet isn't eliminating all your symptoms, ask yourself the following questions:

• Are you following the diet with complete accuracy? There are no gray areas here. Every mistake you make can set you back for up to two days.

• Are you eating five small meals a day, around three hours apart?

• Are you sticking firmly to the amounts indicated in the meal plans or eating less but never more?

If you're absolutely sure you're doing all of the above, you may have personal food allergies or intolerances. They may include the following:

• Chemical substances in foods, whether naturally occurring or added—these include salicylates, which are found in plants (they serve as a natural immune hormone and preservative); benzoates, which are found in food preservatives; penicillin; yeast; and tartrazine (a type of yellow food dye).

• Common food allergens, such as eggs, fish, seafood, and nuts

• Foods in the nightshade family, such as potatoes, eggplant, bell peppers, and tomatoes—they contain glycoalkaloids, a natural pesticide that protects the plant from being eaten by animals.

If you've tried removing each of these possible triggers one by one but still have symptoms, talk to your doctor about being checked for the following conditions:

- Small intestinal bacterial overgrowth (SIBO). This is a proliferation of the wrong kind of gut bacteria. If you do have SIBO, you'll need a course of antibiotics. You should still continue eating low-FODMAP, though, because SIBO will recur if you stop the diet.

- Inflammatory bowel disease (IBD), such as Crohn's disease or colitis. However, this is less likely: These conditions involve inflammation of the bowel, and you would be quite sick if you had them. Doctors always test for them before giving an IBS diagnosis. Still, if you do have IBD, you will probably be advised to stay on a low-FODMAP diet, but you will need extra care from your health practitioner.

- Gut infection—the low-FODMAP diet will not remove the symptoms of a gut infection. Getting tested is relatively easy: do so in order to exclude this possibility. If you do have an infection, you'll probably need a course of antibiotics. Your doctor will guide you on which treatment to follow.

- Gallbladder issues—the symptoms of gallbladder problems are similar to those of IBS. Talk to your doctor about this possibility if the low-FODMAP diet isn't working for you.

Breakfast	VEGGIE RICE WITH POACHED EGGS (page 65) *or* 1 to 2 eggs, 1 cup (90 g) cabbage, and 1 cup (165 g) cooked rice *plus* 10 raspberries *and* weak tea or coffee (optional)
Morning Snack	2 PIZZA MUFFINS (page 68) *or* ½ cup (40 g) mature cheese, up to 20 small rice crackers, and 1 tomato *and* 1 cup (235 ml) lactose-free milk
Lunch	Leftover dinner recipe of your choice *or* 1 filet of fish, 1 cup (70 g) broccoli florets, and 1 cup (138 g) polenta *plus* ½ cup (80 g) cantaloupe *and* a glass of water
Afternoon Snack	1 slice of COFFEE AND WALNUT CAKE (page 72), ¾ cup (170 g) lactose-free yogurt, ½ cup (44 g) sliced fennel *or* up to 20 small rice crackers, ½ cup (44 g) sliced fennel, and ¾ cup (170 g) lactose-free yogurt *and* a glass of water
Dinner	ALMOND AND ROSEMARY CHICKEN WITH SWEET POTATO MASH AND SPINACH (page 79) *or* 1 chicken breast, ½ cup (55 g) sweet potato, and 1 cup (30 g) spinach *and* a glass of water

Notes:

- While recipes have been suggested for the meal plans, feel free to choose an alternative from this week's recipes or those in week one.
- Eggs are high fat so you may only be able to tolerate one at a time.
- Tomatoes should be avoided if you have reflux, so have ½ cup (60 g) zucchini instead.

CRANBERRY AND ALMOND MUESLI

SERVES 12

Muesli is a great breakfast staple, and it's so convenient for busy mornings. Oats are high-fiber and may be too harsh for you, especially if you have IBS with diarrhea, so be sure to test your tolerance levels. On the other hand, though, oats can be an effective tool if you have IBS with constipation. Vary the nuts (no cashews or pistachios) and spices according to taste and serve with lactose-free milk, a low-FODMAP fruit, and lactose-free yogurt.

3 cups (240 g) instant oats

1 cup (120 g) dried cranberries

1 cup (110 g) toasted almond flakes

½ tablespoon (4 g) cinnamon

½ tablespoon (3 g) allspice

Simply combine all the ingredients well and store in an airtight container for up to 1 month.

PANCAKES WITH CANTALOUPE AND YOGURT

SERVES 2

Just because you're eating low-FODMAP doesn't mean you can't enjoy pancakes, everyone's favorite breakfast treat. These pancakes hold together well, so they can be made quite thin. (Replace the cantaloupe with any low-FODMAP fruit, if you like.) Make a few extra pancakes, then serve them for lunch with a protein and a vegetable, such as ½ cup (25 g) of bean sprouts or 2 slices of beetroot.

WEEK TWO
Breakfast

2.9 ounces (83 g) white rice flour

0.7 ounces (21 g) tapioca flour

0.7 ounces (21 g) potato starch

Pinch of salt

1 egg, lightly beaten

1 cup (235 ml) lactose-free milk

½ tablespoon (7 g) butter

1 cup (160 g) chopped cantaloupe

1 cup (230 g) plain lactose-free yogurt

Sift the flours and salt together. Add the lightly beaten egg and mix until well combined. Slowly add the milk, mixing well in between additions.

Melt the butter in a skillet. Pour a thin layer of the pancake mixture into the base of the skillet, tilting the skillet so that the batter spreads evenly. When bubbles form all over the pancake, flip it over and cook on the other side. Repeat with the remaining mixture. Top each pancake with the cantaloupe and yogurt. Store leftover pancakes in the fridge for up to 2 to 3 days or freeze for 2 to 3 months.

VEGGIE RICE WITH POACHED EGGS

SERVES 4

This vegetarian breakfast is a handy way to use up leftover cooked rice and vegetables. It only takes a few minutes to pull together, but to speed up prep even more, you can prepare the vegetables the night before. It constitutes a balanced low-FODMAP meal, and you can have up to a quarter of the recipe at a sitting.

1 tablespoon (15 ml) light olive oil

2 spring onions, thinly sliced
(green parts only)

1 square inch (2.5 square cm)
fresh gingerroot, grated

2 cups (180 g) chopped cabbage

1 carrot, diced

Kernels from 1 cob of fresh corn

1 cup (70 g) small broccoli florets

4 cups (660 g) cooked white or brown rice

2 tablespoons (30 ml) soy sauce

½ tablespoon (7 ml) fish sauce

4 eggs

Salt and pepper

Heat the oil in a skillet. Add the spring onions and ginger. Cook for 1 minute. Add the prepared vegetables and cook for 3 to 4 minutes. Add the rice, stir, and cook until the rice is toasted. Add the soy sauce and fish sauce and mix well.

Poach the eggs for 2 to 3 minutes until the whites are cooked but the yolks are still soft. Divide the rice mixture between bowls and place an egg on top of each. Season to taste and serve immediately. Consume leftovers within 1 day.

EGGPLANT DIP

SERVES 4

This flavorful spiced dip works well as the vegetable for one of your daily snacks. Spread it on low-FODMAP bread or crackers and add a protein, such as a slice of cheese.

1 eggplant/aubergine

1 teaspoon ground cumin

1 teaspoon paprika

1 tablespoon (15 ml) olive oil

1 teaspoon lemon juice

1 tablespoon (6 g) finely sliced spring onions (green part only)

1 tablespoon (6 g) chopped fresh mint

1 tablespoon (14 g) garlic- and onion-free mayonnaise

Salt and pepper

Preheat the oven to 350°F (180°C, or gas mark 4). Cut the aubergine lengthwise into 4 slices and place on a baking sheet. Sprinkle with the cumin and paprika and drizzle the olive oil over the slices. Bake for about 20 minutes or until the flesh is soft. Remove from the oven, let cool slightly, and place in a food processor. Add the rest of the ingredients and process until the mixture forms a smooth paste. Serve immediately. Store leftovers in the fridge for 2 to 3 days.

THAI CHICKEN BALLS

SERVES 7 TO 10

These Asian-inspired chicken balls take next to no time to throw together. In just a few minutes, you'll have a hot, savory snack—or even the protein component of a lunch or dinner. Eat two or three of these with rice crackers and a low-FODMAP vegetable, such as ½ cup (44 g) fennel or 1 cup (35 g) of arugula, for a complete snack. Or serve them to guests as nibbles alongside a glass of wine.

14 ounces (400 g) minced cooked chicken

½ cup (50 g) celery, finely chopped

2 tablespoons (2 g) finely chopped fresh cilantro

1 red chile, finely chopped (omit for reflux)

Grated rind of 1 lemon

½ cup (60 g) low-FODMAP breadcrumbs

¾ teaspoon salt

½ teaspoon black pepper

Preheat the oven to 350°F (180°C, or gas mark 4). Combine all the ingredients in a bowl. Wet your hands and form the mixture into 20 small balls of equal size. Place on a baking sheet lined with parchment paper and bake for 10 minutes until cooked through. Remove from the oven and eat hot or cold. Store leftovers in the fridge for 2 to 3 days or freeze for 1 to 2 months.

PIZZA MUFFINS

Crisp on the outside and deliciously soft in the middle, two of these muffins constitutes a well-balanced snack—once you add a vegetable to them, that is. (I suggest 12 green beans or 1 cup [70 g] of broccoli.) They're perfect when you're on the go. Grab one straight from the freezer and pop it in the microwave for a few seconds to reheat.

1⅓ cups (210 g) white rice flour

⅓ cup (42 g) tapioca flour

⅓ cup (64 g) potato starch

2 teaspoons (9 g) baking powder

Pinch of salt

1.8 ounces (50 g) butter, cut into pieces

1 tablespoon (3 g) chopped fresh basil

1½ cup (150 g) grated mature cheese,
    such as Parmesan

1 egg

1½ cups (352 ml) lactose-free milk

2.6 ounces (75 g) preservative-free
    chopped ham

½ tomato, deseeded and diced
    (omit for reflux)

Preheat the oven to 350°F (180°C, or gas mark 4). Sift the flours, potato starch, baking powder, and salt together. Rub the butter into the dry ingredients with clean fingers. Add the basil and grated cheese and mix to combine. Beat the egg and milk together and add to the mixture and then add the ham and tomato (if using).

Butter or oil a 16-capacity muffin pan well—gluten-free flours tend to stick more than wheat flours. Fill each cup almost to the top. Bake for 20 minutes. Let cool slightly in the pan before removing. Serve warm or cold. Store leftovers in the fridge for 2 to 3 days or freeze for 2 to 3 months.

BLUEBERRY AND LEMON CURD TARTS

MAKES 8 SMALL TARTS

The pastry shells for these summery, citrusy tarts are so versatile. Use them with different fillings and amaze your friends and family with your pastry skills every time. Replace the yogurt topping with a little whipped cream, if you like, but have only one small tart per sitting to stay within safe FODMAP limits.

For the pastry
4.7 ounces (133 g) white rice flour
0.8 ounces (22 g) tapioca flour
1.6 ounces (45 g) potato starch
Pinch of salt
1 heaped (13 g) tablespoon sugar
3.5 ounces (100 g) butter
1 medium egg

For the filling
2 eggs plus 2 egg yolks
¾ cup (150 g) sugar
⅓ cup (75 g) butter
Zest and juice of 2 lemons

For the topping
Blueberries
Plain lactose-free yogurt

First, prepare the pastry. Preheat the oven to 350°F (180°C, or gas mark 4). Blend all the dry ingredients in a food processor. Cut the butter into small pieces, add to the food processor, and process until fine crumbs form. Add the egg and process until the mixture forms a dough. Remove from the processor. Add a little more rice flour if it is too wet. (This will depend on the size of your eggs.) Press the pastry into eight 3-in (7.5 cm) greased tart pans (or four larger ones) and place in the fridge for 30 minutes.

Remove the pans from the fridge. Place a circle of parchment paper on top of each round of dough, fill each pan with rice or dried beans, and blind bake for 5 minutes. Remove the paper and rice or beans and cook for another 10 minutes. Cover with aluminum foil if the edges start to burn. Remove from the oven and let cool.

Meanwhile, prepare the filling. Beat the whole eggs and yolks and the sugar in a saucepan and place over a low heat. Once warm, add the butter and stir it until melted. Add the lemon zest and juice and whisk well. Continue whisking until the mixture thickens, about 10 to 15 minutes. Let cool.

Fill each pastry shell with lemon curd and place in the fridge to set, about 2 hours. Place a small dollop of lactose-free yogurt in the middle of each and decorate with blueberries. Store in the fridge for 2 to 3 days.

COFFEE AND WALNUT CAKE

SERVES 12

Thanks to a secret ingredient—mashed potato!—and the right balance of healthy flours, your guests will never guess that there's no wheat in this soft, moist cake. Vary the nuts if you like as long as they are soft: pecans work well, for example. Be careful not overindulge: have a single slice and enjoy every mouthful.

7 ounces (200 g) softened butter

5.5 ounces (150 g) superfine granulated white sugar

4 eggs

1.4 ounces (40 g) white rice flour

1 ounce (25 g) potato starch

0.4 ounces (10 g) tapioca flour

2 teaspoons (9 g) baking powder

2 teaspoons (2 g) instant coffee granules

8.8 ounces (250 g) cooked mashed potato

⅓ cup (40 g) walnut pieces

2.6 ounces (75 g) almond meal

Preheat the oven to 350°F (180°C, or gas mark 4). Butter and line an 8-inch (20 cm) cake pan. Beat the butter and sugar together until light and fluffy. Add the eggs one at a time, beating well after each addition. Sift the rice flour, potato starch, tapioca flour, and baking powder together and add the coffee granules. Add the dry ingredients to the butter mixture. Add the mashed potato, walnuts, and the almond meal. Pour the batter into the pan and bake for 30 minutes or until a skewer comes out clean. Let cool in the pan for 5 to 10 minutes and then turn out onto a wire rack. Cool completely before serving. Store in an airtight container for 1 day on the countertop, 2 to 3 days in the fridge, or freeze for 2 to 3 months.

TUNA, TOMATO, AND RICE STIR-FRY

SERVES 4

If you have leftover rice, you have the makings of a quick, nutritious dinner. Just add a few basic ingredients, and a balanced meal covering all of the food groups will be on the table in minutes. If you have reflux, omit the chile and avoid the tomatoes—use a different low-FOMAP vegetable, such as 2 cups (134 g) of kale or 4 small yellow squash, instead.

1 tablespoon (15 ml) oil

1 spring onion, sliced (green part only)

½ stalk of celery, finely sliced

1 deseeded red chile, chopped finely (omit for reflux)

2 teaspoons (5 g) ground cumin

2 teaspoons (4 g) ground turmeric

4 cups (660 g) cooked rice

6.5 ounces (185 g) canned tuna in spring water, drained

2 tomatoes, chopped (omit for reflux)

3 tablespoons (12 g) chopped fresh parsley

3 tablespoons (45 ml) soy sauce

Heat the oil in a wok. When hot, add the spring onion, celery, chile (if using), cumin, and turmeric and cook for 1 minute. Add the rice and cook until well-coated in the spices. Add the tomatoes (if using) and tuna. Cook 1 to 2 minutes to heat through and add the parsley and soy sauce. Cook 2 minutes more, remove from the heat, and serve immediately.

STUFFED CURRIED LAMB POTATOES

SERVES 4 (1 POTATO/2 HALVES PER SERVING)

This easy, satisfying recipe covers all the food groups and is a meal in itself. Use the starchiest potatoes so that they mash well. Be sure to have only one serving—that is, two halves—to stay within permitted FODMAP levels. You can replace the lamb with any ground meat you like.

4 medium potatoes

1 tablespoon (15 ml) light olive oil

1 teaspoon ground cumin

1 teaspoon cumin seeds

1 teaspoon garam masala

1 teaspoon ground turmeric

1 teaspoon ground coriander

½ teaspoon chile powder (omit for reflux)

2 spring onions, sliced thinly
   (green parts only)

14 ounces (400 g) lean ground lamb

1 zucchini, diced

2 tablespoons (28 g) butter

¼ cup (59 ml) lactose-free milk

1 tablespoon (6 g) finely chopped fresh mint

Salt and pepper

1 cup (120 g) grated mature cheese

Preheat the oven to 350°F (180°C, or gas mark 4). Wash the potatoes and place them in the oven for 1 hour. (You can wrap them in foil, if you like, but the skins will be less crispy.) Heat the oil in a skillet and add the spices and spring onions. Cook 1 minute. Add the ground lamb and cook until almost cooked through. Add the zucchini and cook for 3 to 4 minutes more.

When the potatoes are soft, remove them from the oven. Handling them carefully (they are hot), slice them in half lengthwise and remove most of the potato flesh with a spoon. Place the flesh in a large bowl and mash with the butter and milk. Add the ground lamb mixture and mint to the potato flesh. Mix well and season to taste. Pile the mixture back into the potato shells and top each with the cheese. Place in the oven for 5 to 10 minutes or until the cheese melts. Serve immediately. Store leftovers in the fridge for up to 2 days.

FENNEL, WALNUT, AND BRIE TART

SERVES 4 TO 6

Tarts like this one make great light dinners. Plus, there are usually leftovers for lunch the next day. This elegant vegetarian dish covers all the food groups, so it's a complete meal—and it's so good that it'll even satisfy non-vegetarians. Take it along as your contribution to a shared meal or potluck supper.

WEEK TWO
Dinners

For the pastry

4.7 ounces (133 g) white rice flour

0.8 ounces (22 g) tapioca flour

1.6 ounces (45 g) potato starch

Pinch of salt

3.5 ounces (100 g) butter

1 medium egg

For the filling

1 wedge (7 ounces, 196 g) of
    Brie cheese, sliced

1 fennel bulb, sliced

1 cup (120 g) toasted walnuts

2 eggs

5.7 ounces (170 ml) lactose-free milk

1 heaped tablespoon (15 g) cottage cheese

1 tablespoon (4 g) finely chopped
    fresh oregano

Salt and pepper

First, prepare the pastry. Preheat the oven to 350°F (180°C, or gas mark 4). Blend all the dry ingredients in a food processor. Cut the butter into small pieces, add to the food processor, and process until fine crumbs form. Add the egg and process until the mixture forms a dough. Remove from the processor and add a little more rice flour if it is too wet (this will depend on the size of your egg). Press the pastry into a 10-in (26 cm) greased tart pan and place in the fridge for 30 minutes.

Place a circle of parchment paper on top of the dough, fill with raw rice or dried beans, and blind bake for 5 minutes. Remove the paper and rice or beans and cook for another 10 minutes. Cover with aluminum foil if the edges start to burn. Remove from the oven and let cool.

Press the slices of cheese into the base of the tart. Cover with the fennel and nuts. Beat the eggs into the milk. Add the cottage cheese and stir. Then add the oregano and mix well. Pour the mixture into the tart pan (depending on the depth of your tart pan, there may be a little left over: don't overfill). Bake for 20 minutes or until the custard is set. Cover the pastry edges with aluminum foil if necessary. Remove from the oven. Season to taste and eat piping hot. Store leftovers in the fridge for 2 to 3 days or freeze for 2 to 3 months.

BEEF TACOS WITH SPINACH

SERVES 4

Taco shells made from corn are naturally low-FODMAP. That means you can have up to two of these filling, spicy beef tacos at a sitting. Use 2 cups (110 g) of salad leaves or lettuce instead of the spinach or change up the meat and use pork or chicken instead of beef. If you don't have an issue with lactose, you could use sour cream instead of the lactose-free yogurt, too.

WEEK TWO
Dinners

1 tablespoon (15 ml) light olive oil

1 teaspoon ground turmeric

1 teaspoon ground cumin

1 teaspoon cumin seeds

1 teaspoon paprika

14 ounces (400 g) ground beef

½ cup (117 ml) water or garlic- and onion-free beef or chicken stock

1 tablespoon (8 g) low-FODMAP flour (such as tapioca or corn flour)

Salt and pepper

8 corn taco shells

2 tomatoes, diced (omit for reflux)

2 cups (60 g) baby spinach

1 cup (50 g) bean sprouts

Plain lactose-free yogurt

Preheat the oven to 350°F (180°C, or gas mark 4). Heat the oil in a skillet and add the spices. Cook for 1 minute to release the flavors. Add the ground beef and cook until browned and cooked through. Add the water or stock and flour to the ground beef and cook until a thick sauce forms, about 3 to 4 minutes. Season to taste.

Warm the taco shells for 5 minutes in the preheated oven. Place the ground beef mixture in the base of the shells and then top with all the other ingredients. Serve immediately.

ALMOND AND ROSEMARY CHICKEN WITH SWEET POTATO MASH AND SPINACH

SERVES 4

Healthy, colorful, and flavorful, this meal is a template for a well-balanced low-FODMAP dinner. The sweet potato could be replaced by 2 cups (450 g) of pumpkin, or even 4 cups (660 g) of cooked rice, and the spinach could be replaced by 4 cups (268 g) of kale. If you want to use less oil, then drizzle a little olive oil over the chicken filets and bake in the oven instead.

2 chicken breasts

1 tablespoon (10 g) white rice flour

3 heaped tablespoons (about 25 g) low-FODMAP breadcrumbs

1 tablespoon (2 g) finely chopped rosemary

1 tablespoon (7 g) finely chopped almonds

1 teaspoon paprika

Salt and pepper

1 egg

2 sweet potatoes (about 10 ounces or 280 g total)

2 tablespoons (30 ml) light olive oil

1 tablespoon (14 g) butter

¼ cup (25 g) grated mature cheese, such as Parmesan

1 bunch (4 cups or 120 g) of spinach leaves, washed, tough stalks removed

Slice each chicken breast through the middle lengthways to form two flat filets. Cover each filet with plastic wrap and flatten them a little more by beating with a rolling pin. Place the flour in a plate and season it. Dredge each filet in the flour, covering it completely. Shake off any excess flour.

Mix the breadcrumbs, rosemary, almonds, paprika, salt, and pepper together. Beat the egg in a shallow bowl. Dunk the floured filets in the egg. Make sure they are completely covered. Let any excess egg drip off. Dredge each of the filets in the breadcrumb mixture, pressing it into the meat. Place in the fridge for 5 minutes to firm up.

Meanwhile, peel and cut up the sweet potatoes. Place in salted water and boil until soft. Drain and set aside.

Heat the olive oil in a large skillet. When the oil is hot, add the chicken filets. Cook until browned on both sides and cooked through. (Exact cooking time depends on the thickness of your filets, but it usually only takes a couple minutes per side.)

Add the butter and cheese to the sweet potatoes and mash well. When the chicken is almost done, place a little water in a large saucepan and heat. When hot, steam the spinach until wilted (about 3 to 4 minutes). Season to taste. Serve the chicken alongside the mashed sweet potato and wilted spinach.

BREADED MUSSELS

SERVES 3 TO 4

Mussels consist mainly of protein, so they are unlimited from a FODMAP point of view. These are topped with a cheesy, breadcrumb seasoning before being baked, and they're delicious. Eat them with 1 cup (138 g) of mashed potatoes or ½ cup (55 g) of mashed sweet potatoes and a low-FODMAP vegetable, such as 6 pods of okra or ½ cup (41 g) of eggplant. If you prefer, you can skip the breadcrumbs and eat the mussels right after steaming.

1.75 pounds (800 g) mussels

1 tablespoon (15 ml) light olive oil

1 tablespoon (15 ml) white wine

1.8 ounces (50 g) Parmesan cheese, grated

1.8 ounces (50 g) low-FODMAP breadcrumbs

Black pepper

1 tablespoon (4 g) finely chopped fresh parsley, plus more for serving

Olive oil

Preheat the oven to 350°F (180°C, or gas mark 4). Clean the mussels thoroughly and remove the beards.

Heat the oil in a saucepan, add the mussels, and cover. When they open, add the white wine. Cook until the wine burns off, about 2 to 3 minutes.

Remove the mussels from the heat and discard those that didn't open. Remove the mussels from the shells, keeping just one side of each shell. Discard the rest. Reserve some of the cooking liquid: filter through cheesecloth to remove any grit.

In a bowl, mix the Parmesan, breadcrumbs, pepper, and parsley with some of the cooking liquid, just until the mixture is damp. Place each mussel on a shell and cover with a couple teaspoons of the breadcrumb mixture and a drizzle of olive oil. Arrange on a baking sheet, place in the oven for 15 minutes, and then switch to the broiler and let them brown on the top. Garnish with chopped parsley and serve immediately.

PESTO AND CHICKEN PIZZA

SERVES 4

Kneading the dough for this unusual pizza crust takes a bit of effort, but the result is a thin, crispy crust that's perfect for a variety of low-FODMAP toppings. If you have reflux, skip the bell pepper and replace it with an alternate vegetable—like zucchini, perhaps.

For the pesto sauce

2 cups (48 g) basil leaves

1½ tablespoons (14 g) pine nuts

1.4 ounces (40 g) Parmesan cheese

1 teaspoon garlic-infused oil
    (omit for reflux)

Olive oil

Salt

For the pizza crust

1 cup (128 g) tapioca flour, divided

5 tablespoons (75 ml) water

2 tablespoons (30 ml) light olive oil, divided

½ teaspoon baking soda

¼ teaspoon salt

1 teaspoon cumin seeds

1 egg

For the toppings

Pesto sauce

1 cup (140 g) chopped cooked chicken

½ red bell pepper, diced (omit for reflux)

1 cup (120 g) grated mature cheese,
    such as Cheddar

First, prepare the pesto sauce. Place the basil, pine nuts, and cheese into a food processor and process until finely chopped. Add the garlic oil (if using) and then add 1 tablespoon (15 ml) of olive oil at a time, pulsing between additions, until the right consistency is achieved (a thick, spoonable paste). Season with salt to taste and set aside.

Then, prepare the dough. Preheat the oven to 350°F (180°C, or gas mark 4). Place ⅓ cup (42 g) of the tapioca flour, the water, and 1 tablespoon (15 ml) of the olive oil in a small saucepan. Heat on low, stirring, until the mixture sticks together well. Remove from the heat and let cool.

In a bowl, combine the rest of the flour, the baking soda, salt, and cumin seeds. Add the egg and the rest of the oil and mix. Add the cooled congealed flour mixture and knead together well into a dough. Push the dough out into a flat, round shape on a baking sheet lined with parchment paper.

Bake until almost crisp on one side, about 20 minutes, and then flip over and repeat. (This time, the crust will take less time to brown; keep an eye on it.) Remove from the oven and assemble the pizza immediately: Spread the pesto sauce onto the prepared crust, followed by the chicken and bell pepper (if using). Season to taste and then scatter with the grated cheese. Return to the oven until the cheese is melted, about 3 to 5 minutes. Serve hot. Store in an airtight container in the fridge for 2 to 3 days.

POTATO AND SPINACH SOUP

SERVES 4

This thick, hearty soup constitutes a complete meal. Have around a quarter of the recipe—but don't go back to the pot for a second helping or you could exceed your FODMAP limit for one meal. If you prefer a country-style soup, skip the pureeing and leave it chunky.

1 tablespoon (15 ml) light olive oil

½ stalk of celery, finely chopped

1 red chile, finely chopped (omit for reflux)

1 knob of gingerroot (1 inch, or 2.5 cm), peeled and finely chopped

1 teaspoon ground cumin

4 white potatoes, peeled and cut into large cubes

20 green beans, cut into 1-inch (2.5 cm) pieces

17 ounces (500 ml) garlic- and onion-free chicken stock

½ cup (125 g) tomato puree (omit for reflux)

2 cups (60 g) spinach, chopped

8 slices of lean bacon, cut into bite-sized pieces (omit for a vegetarian dish)

Paprika

Chopped fresh mint

Heat the oil in a large saucepan and add the celery, chile (if using), and ginger. Sauté for 1 minute and then add the cumin and cook for 30 seconds more. Add the potatoes and green beans to the ginger mix, toss, and cook for a few minutes, stirring continuously. Add the stock and tomato puree (if using) and cook, covered, until the vegetables are almost cooked through. Add the spinach and allow it to wilt down.

Meanwhile, cook the bacon (if using) in a little oil until crisp.

When the spinach has wilted into the soup, place a little more than half of the soup into a food processor and blend until smooth. Add the blended soup back to the saucepan with the rest of the soup and reheat. Serve in bowls and garnish each with a quarter of the bacon, a sprinkling of paprika, and chopped mint.

DIARY PAGE | **WEEK TWO** | DATE ___/___/___

SLEEP _____ hours   from _____ to _____

Quality of sleep _____

_____

_____

_____

RELAXATION _____ minutes   from _____ to _____

Type _____

_____

_____

_____

BOWEL MOVEMENTS _____ number   times _____

Type* _____

_____

_____

_____

MEDICATION

Type _____

_____

_____

_____

SUPPLEMENTS

Type _____   _____

_____   _____

_____   _____

_____   _____

*To find what type of bowel movement you've had, search the Internet for "Bristol Stool Chart."

FOOD JOURNAL | WEEK TWO

MEAL	TIME	NOTES/SYMPTOMS
Breakfast _____	_____	_____
_____	_____	_____
_____	_____	_____
_____	_____	_____
_____	_____	_____
_____	_____	_____
Morning snack _____	_____	_____
_____	_____	_____
_____	_____	_____
_____	_____	_____
Lunch _____	_____	_____
_____	_____	_____
_____	_____	_____
_____	_____	_____
_____	_____	_____
_____	_____	_____
Afternoon snack _____	_____	_____
_____	_____	_____
_____	_____	_____
_____	_____	_____
Dinner _____	_____	_____
_____	_____	_____
_____	_____	_____
_____	_____	_____
_____	_____	_____
_____	_____	_____

Lifestyle Exercise: **RELAXATION**

There will always be a degree of stress in your life, but the good news is that relaxation techniques can help counter the buildup of adrenaline that's released during stress and bring you back to a state of calm. Relaxation reduces stress, which can lead to a number of benefits including lowering the risk of high blood pressure, depression, and even catching a cold.

PREFERRED RELAXATION TECHNIQUE: RHYTHMIC BREATHING

When you are stressed, your heart rate increases, adrenaline floods your body, and your breathing becomes shallow and fast. We can't control our heart rates or the presence of adrenalin, but we can control our breathing rates. Slow, rhythmic breaths will fool the body into thinking that no stressful situation exists after all: the heart will slow down and the tide of adrenaline will recede. This de-stressing method can be used anywhere, anytime, and you should use it whenever you're feeling stressed.

Your Exercise This Week:

- Schedule relaxation time for 10 minutes every day.

- Find a quiet place without distractions or noise.

- Sit or lie down in a comfortable position. (Don't lie down if this tends to send you to sleep.)

- Focus on your breathing, concentrating on making it slow and rhythmic for the full 10 minutes.

Over time, this exercise will form a pathway in your brain, which will make it easier for you to remember to do this when you are stressed. Be consistent and this will happen within a couple of weeks. Once you find yourself doing rhythmic breathing automatically when stressed, you no longer need to do the daily ten-minute routine.

Diet Integration:
STAND UP FOR YOURSELF

Now that you're on the right path to good health, you must learn to stand up for yourself and not to let anyone undermine you or set you back on this transformative path. Never, never apologize for trying to get healthy. Having a solid goal instills confidence and gives you a sense of purpose that should prevent others from walking all over you.

When you feel the vibes of scepticism from another person concerning your diet, the first thing you should do is observe your body language.

- Don't slump or fidget.

- Stand or sit tall and stay still.

- Look the person directly in the eye while they speak and don't move until they've finished.

- Make sure your body language is open and not closed: no crossed arms or legs.

Then, focus on your speech.

- Don't interrupt: Let them say their piece. When it is your turn to speak, make sure they don't interrupt you, either.

- When you respond, use "I" and not "you:" There should be no accusations. That will just put the other person on the defensive. Don't let the word "you" creep into your discourse.

- Speak slowly, clearly, and with a tone of authority: Do not mumble or speak in a quiet voice. What you are saying is not up for discussion, so drop your voice at the end of your sentences and especially at the end of your speech. Don't leave any room for an upward or querulous inflection in your voice. You are an authority figure where you and your health are concerned. Don't leave that in any doubt. Command respect.

Bullies—and we all have them in our lives—are used to people giving way before them, so stand your ground and calmly wait for them to finish speaking. Stay open, understanding, and confident. If they continue to rant, walk away. Don't let yourself be bullied.

If you tend to be a "yes" person, then you have to learn how to say "no." When someone presses a second glass of wine on you, say no and mean it, leaving no room for doubt in your body language and tone of voice. If you demonstrate your confidence and conviction in your aim, you are less likely to be questioned about your decisions. And, while you are learning to behave in an assertive way, follow the old saying: Fake it until you make it. You'll get there.

MARYANN

For Maryann, it took a little longer than a week to get her symptoms under control on the program. When she did, she was ecstatic. Every new day was better than the previous one.

But, on the day before we were to start the reintroduction stage of the diet, Maryann emailed me in desperation. Her diarrhea had returned, completely out of the blue. She swore she had followed the diet religiously, like always. We had a phone consultation booked for later in the day, so I told her to do her deep breathing exercise for a few minutes each hour for the rest of the day and that we'd talk more during our call. Once we connected, she said that the diarrhea had stopped and she was feeling fine. I asked her about her stress levels during the day. She told me that she'd had a relaxing day at home getting ready for Christmas, which was a week away.

I was still bamboozled: I couldn't figure out why she'd had such an episode. As we continued talking, she began to tell me that she had received a Christmas card in the mail that day from her stepdaughter, with whom she didn't get along. She said that her stepdaughter had included a comment in the card that was meant as a deliberate dig at her. I interrupted her story and asked her if that had been upsetting to her. Maryann gasped and said, "I still had the card in my hand when I rushed to the toilet with diarrhea." She admitted that she hadn't even seen the connection between her stressful experience and her symptoms. But the truth was that stress had completely undermined her clean low-FODMAP diet and caused a return of symptoms—even though, fortunately, they were short-lived.

Since then, Maryann has been aware of the way in which stress can affect her symptoms. She uses relaxation techniques to deal with stress when it hits, and she feels better than ever.

WEEK THREE

Stay the Course
Getting Ready for Testing

If you have been following the diet accurately, your symptoms should be long gone by now. But that doesn't mean your job is done. Now is the time to dig deep and stay the course—especially because this is often when you start to fool yourself into thinking that perhaps there was nothing wrong with you in the first place. How could you feel this good *and* have a permanent condition? Don't let the cream cake or chocolate bar tempt you into testing your theory, though. I assure you that the punishment for turning your back on your IBS is not worth it. Stay strong.

By now, even people with constipation should be having bowel movements that look like numbers three and four on the Bristol Stool chart, a chart that divides the different types of bowel movements into seven different categories ranging from constipated to diarrhea. However, now is a good time to talk about what may constitute "normal" for people with IBS.

The usual number of times to visit the toilet each day is between one and three. So if you're going a few times a day, there's no need to worry, as long as the stool itself is of a good consistency. You may also skip a day every now and then, and that's fine, too.

When you go to the toilet—especially if you're constipated—you might have to sit there for a little while before anything happens. Don't strain, or you're going to end up with hemorrhoids and maybe even anal fissures (tears in the lining of the anus). So don't rush: You need to have a peaceful stretch of time in front of you. Make sure your feet are elevated; this straightens out the colon so that there's no kink in it. Bring a box or small pile of books into the bathroom so you have something to prop your feet on and then sit and wait for it to happen. If you're going to the toilet regularly at the same time every day—and hopefully the first time is straight after breakfast—then your body will come to know when to expect a visit to the toilet and will perform.

Unfortunately, a feeling of incomplete evacuation is one of the symptoms of IBS, especially if you're constipated—but often there's nothing left to come out. The feeling may be a result of one of those false messages from the brain discussed in chapter 1. So, simply let your body relax back into its normal position while you're still on the toilet, so that you start to feel comfortable while you're sitting there, and then stand up. As long as you keep straining, you will continue to feel that there's more stool to come. Stop straining, stop pushing, and wait.

Finally, testing is just ahead of you. That's exciting, but it can also be a little daunting—so for now, enjoy this week of being relatively symptom-free.

WEEK THREE

Breakfast	BLUEBERRY AND PEANUT BUTTER OATMEAL (page 93) and 2 radishes *or* 1 tablespoon (16 g) peanut butter, ¼ cup (20 g) oats (raw measurement), 1 cup (235 ml) lactose-free milk, 2 radishes, and 2 tablespoons (30 g) lactose-free yogurt *plus* ¼ cup (37 g) blueberries *and* weak tea or coffee (optional)
Morning Snack	3 to 4 BEEF AND RED PEPPER PIZZETTAS (page 96) *or* 2 ounces (60 g) beef, up to 20 small rice crackers, and ½ cup (75 g) red pepper *and* 1 cup (235 ml) lactose-free milk
Lunch	Leftover dinner recipe *or* 1 chicken filet, 1 cup (30 g) spinach, and ½ cup (55 g) sweet potato *plus* 1 barely-ripe banana *and* a glass of water
Afternoon Snack	1 CRANBERRY MUESLI BAR (page 102), ¾ cup (170 g) lactose-free yogurt, 2 slices of beet *or* up to 20 small rice crackers, 2 slices of beet, and ¾ cup (170 g) lactose-free yogurt *and* a glass of water
Dinner	TUNA PASTA SALAD WITH SNOW PEAS AND RADISHES (page 107) *or* 1 fish filet, 5 snow peas, and 1 cup (107 g) cooked low-FODMAP pasta *and* a glass of water

Notes:

- While recipes have been suggested for the meal plans, feel free to choose an alternative from this week's recipes or those in week one or two.
- Even though we can have up to 2 tablespoons (32 g) of peanut butter from a FODMAP point of view, that is a high amount of oil to consume at once so stick to 1 tablespoon (16 g) or less.
- If you have reflux, avoid the red pepper and perhaps have 1 carrot instead.

BLUEBERRY AND PEANUT BUTTER OATMEAL

SERVES 4

Oats are relatively high in fiber, so oatmeal is a good breakfast choice for people with constipation. If you have IBS with diarrhea, start with a small portion and see how that goes. If you're not a fan of blueberries, you could add any alternative low-FODMAP fruit instead, and you can drizzle your serving with a little maple syrup for added sweetness. Pair it with a vegetable—such as half of a cob of corn or 1 cup (70 g) of bok choy—to make a balanced meal.

1 cup (80 g) uncooked instant oats

2 cups (470 ml) lactose-free milk

Pinch of salt

4 tablespoons (64 g) peanut butter

3.9 ounces (112 g) blueberries

Place the oats and milk in a saucepan. Bring to a boil. Reduce the heat to low and add the salt. Simmer until thick and creamy, about 5 minutes, stirring continuously to prevent sticking. Stir in the peanut butter and let sit for 5 minutes. Spoon into bowls and serve immediately with the blueberries sprinkled on top.

THREE-CHEESE SPANISH TORTILLA

SERVES 4

It's easy to tailor this hearty, classic omelet to your taste by substituting other low-FODMAP ingredients that appeal to you. For instance, you could add 2 cups (240 g) zucchini or use 2 cups (450 g) sliced pumpkin in place of the potato. It's also suitable for lunch or dinner, and it's a complete meal.

1 tablespoon (14 g) butter

2 teaspoons (10 ml) light olive oil

6 eggs

4 tablespoons (59 ml) lactose-free milk

1 spring onion, finely sliced (green part only)

1 tablespoon (3 g) chopped fresh basil

1 cup (250 g) cubed feta cheese

⅓ cup (40 g) mature cheese,
    such as Cheddar

⅓ cup (38 g) grated Parmesan cheese

Salt and pepper, to taste

1 large cooked potato, sliced

2 cups (288 g) mixed salad leaves

Preheat the broiler in the oven. Heat the butter and oil in a large ovenproof skillet. Break the eggs into a bowl, add the milk, and beat them together. Add the spring onion, basil, feta, Cheddar, and Parmesan and fold through. Season to taste. Pour the mixture into the oiled skillet. Lay the potato slices all over the egg mixture and press down slightly.

As the tortilla cooks, use a spatula to pull in the edges a little to let the uncooked egg run underneath. When the bottom is set, place the pan into the oven about halfway down and leave until the top is set. Remove from the oven and scatter the salad leaves over the tortilla. Serve hot. Store leftovers in the fridge for 2 to 3 days.

MINI KALE MUFFINS

SERVES 8

This quick vegetarian recipe makes breakfast for the whole family in minutes. These muffins will keep in the fridge for a few days—or, you could make the mixture ahead of time, store it in the fridge for a day or two, and then bake them as required. Feel free to swap the kale for a similar vegetable, such as spinach, bok choy, or zucchini.

8 eggs
⅔ cup (153 g) plain lactose-free yogurt
2 cups (134 g) finely chopped kale
½ cup (50 g) grated Parmesan cheese
Salt and pepper

Preheat the oven to 350°F (180°C, or gas mark 4). Oil four 12-cup mini muffin pans. Beat the eggs with the yogurt and then add the kale and cheese. Season to taste. Divide the mixture between the muffin pans, filling each cup three-quarters full. Bake for 15 minutes or until set and cooked through. Let cool for a few minutes and then turn them out onto a wire rack and serve hot or cold. Store leftovers in the fridge for 3 to 4 days.

BEEF AND RED PEPPER PIZZETTAS

SERVES 4

These miniature pizzas make delicious snacks—three or four constitute a balanced snack. You can also serve them to friends as nibbles alongside drinks. Replace the meat with a different protein of your choice, if you like, or use grilled tofu for a satisfying vegetarian dish. Eat them within the same day.

For the pizzettas

1½ cups (192 g) tapioca flour

1½ cups (237 g) white rice flour

1 teaspoon salt

⅓ cup (80 ml) light olive oil

1 cup (235 ml) water

2 eggs

2 teaspoons (4 g) cumin seeds

For the toppings

4 ounces (120 g) sirloin steak

2 red bell peppers (omit for reflux)

1 teaspoon garlic-infused oil
   (omit for reflux)

1 tablespoon (15 ml) olive oil

1 tablespoon (4 g) chopped fresh parsley

Salt and pepper

1 cup (250 g) crumbled feta cheese

1 heaped tablespoon (15 g)
   horseradish sauce

First, prepare the pizzetta bases. Preheat the oven to 350°F (180°C, or gas mark 4). Sift the two flours and salt together. Combine the olive oil and water in a small saucepan and bring to a boil. Remove from the heat and add the flour mixture. Mix thoroughly. Add the eggs and cumin seeds and mix to combine into a dough.

Turn the dough out onto a low-FODMAP-floured countertop or worktop and knead the dough into a ball. Divide the dough into 12 pieces and push out into 12 flat round shapes. Place the pizzetta bases on a baking sheet lined with parchment paper. Bake for 15 to 20 minutes until crisp on the outside but soft and slightly gooey inside. Do not overbake.

Prepare the toppings. Grill the steak until medium-rare, let rest for 5 minutes, and then cut against the grain into thin slices. Char the peppers (if using) under the broiler until the skin is black. Remove the skins. Slice the peppers and then mix with the garlic oil, the olive oil, and the parsley. Season with salt and pepper.

Scatter an equal amount of feta on top of each of the pizzetta bases. Place under the broiler for 2 to 3 minutes or until hot. Place a dollop of the pepper mixture on top of the hot feta and add 1 to 2 slices of steak. Place a ½ teaspoon of horseradish in the middle of the steak. Serve immediately.

CHEESE BALLS

SERVES 4

This simple vegetarian dish combines a variety of permitted cheeses. The total amount of cheese in a serving is under the permitted level of lactose, as is the amount of almond meal. For a complete snack, have four or five of these with low-FODMAP crackers and a selection of vegetable sticks, such as fennel, carrots, zucchini, and snow peas. You could also roll the balls in chopped nuts, such as walnuts or pecans.

7 ounces (200 g) feta, finely chopped

3 tablespoons (42 g) cottage cheese

3 tablespoons (45 g) cream cheese

3 tablespoons (15 g) grated
　Parmesan cheese

3 tablespoons (18 g) almond meal

1 teaspoon paprika

½ cup (30 g) finely chopped fresh parsley

Mix everything together in a bowl except the parsley. Roll the mixture into 16 balls and then roll each in the chopped parsley. Place on a serving dish and refrigerate for a few hours before serving. Store in the fridge for 3 to 4 days.

BANANA CAKE

SERVES 12

This moist, easy-to-make cake is just as easy to eat, but don't overindulge. Stick to one small slice at a time. You could put a simple frosting on it if you like—such as the frosting on the Chocolate and Orange Polenta Cake (page 42)—especially if you have guests. Slice up leftovers into individual portion sizes and freeze them. Then, defrost them in a microwave for 20 to 30 seconds as needed.

4.4 ounces (125 g) softened butter

1 cup (200 g) superfine granulated white sugar

¼ cup (60 g) brown sugar

3 eggs

1⅓ cups (210 g) white rice flour

⅓ cup (42 g) tapioca flour

⅓ cup (64 g) potato starch

2 teaspoons (9 g) baking powder

1 teaspoon cinnamon

¾ cup (173 g) plain lactose-free yogurt

1 cup (225 g) mashed just ripe banana

Preheat the oven to 350°F (180°C, or gas mark 4). Place the butter and sugars in a bowl and mix with an electric blender until fluffy and pale. Add the eggs one at a time and mix well after each addition.

Sift the dry ingredients together and fold into the butter mixture. Add the yogurt and banana and stir to combine. Spoon the mixture into a buttered, lined cake pan. Bake for 40 minutes or until a toothpick inserted into the center comes out clean. Let cool on a wire rack. Store in an airtight container on the countertop for 1 day; store in the fridge for 2 to 3 days; or freeze for 2 to 3 months.

CHOCOLATE MERINGUE TARTS

SERVES 8

Decadent and chocolaty yet low-FODMAP, these tarts are the ultimate sweet snacks. If you bake them in larger pans, they're great as a special dessert, too. Depending on your tolerance to sugar, start with no more than one small tart and see how you go. Use any leftover meringue to make individual meringues.

For the pastry

4.7 ounces (133 g) white rice flour

0.8 ounces (22 g) tapioca flour

1.6 ounces (45 g) potato starch

Pinch of salt

1 heaped (about 13 g) tablespoon sugar

3.5 ounces (100 g) butter, cut into
   small pieces

1 medium egg

For the filling

1⅓ cups (315 ml) lactose-free milk

¼ cup (50 g) superfine granulated
   white sugar

Pinch of salt

3 egg yolks, lightly beaten

3 ounces (85 g) dark chocolate,
   broken into pieces

For the meringue

3 pasteurized egg whites

2.5 ounces (70 g) superfine granulated
   white sugar

First, prepare the pastry. Preheat the oven to 350°F (180°C, or gas mark 4). Blend all the ingredients in a food processor. Remove the dough from the processor and add a little more rice flour if it is too wet. Press the dough into eight 3-inch (7.5 cm) tart pans or four 4.5-in (11.5 cm) pans. Place a circle of parchment paper on top of each pan of dough, fill with dried beans or rice and blind bake for 5 minutes. Remove the paper and beans or rice, and cook for another 10 minutes. Cover with aluminum foil if the edges start to burn. Remove from the oven and let cool.

Meanwhile, prepare the filling. Heat the milk in a double boiler and then add the sugar and salt. Heat until the sugar is dissolved. Add a couple of tablespoons (30 ml) of the milk mixture to the eggs and mix briskly. Keeping the milk on the heat, add the yolks to the milk. Continue stirring until the mixture thickens a little. Add the chocolate and stir until it dissolves. Keep heating while stirring until the custard coats the back of a metal spoon. Divide the mixture between the pastry shells.

Prepare the meringue. Beat the egg whites with an electric mixer to form soft peaks. Add the sugar one spoonful at a time, beating continuously. Keep beating until stiff peaks form. Pile the meringue onto the tarts. Place the tarts on a baking sheet and place under a broiler (but not too close to it) until the top is toasted. Watch closely as this will happen quickly. Place in the fridge until the custard is set, at least 2 hours. Store in the fridge for 2 to 3 days.

CRANBERRY MUESLI BARS

SERVES 14

Hunger is your enemy when you have IBS, so you always need to keep a snack on hand when you're out and about. That way, you won't be tempted to reach for the wrong foods. These muesli bars will do the trick nicely. Wrap one in a piece of aluminum foil and take it with you as a serving.

WEEK THREE
Sweet Treats

¼ cup (40 g) white rice flour

¼ cup (32 g) tapioca flour

½ teaspoon baking soda

1 teaspoon cinnamon

1 teaspoon ground cardamom

Pinch of salt

1 cup (80 g) rolled oats

½ cup (42 g) desiccated coconut

½ cup (100 g) sugar

¾ cup (90 g) dried cranberries

½ cup (56 g) almond flakes

½ tablespoon (10 g) maple syrup or golden syrup

4.4 ounces (125 g) hot melted butter

Preheat the oven to 350°F (180°C, or gas mark 4). Oil and line an 11- x 7-in (28 x 18 cm) baking sheet. Sift the flours, baking soda, cinnamon, cardamom, and salt together. Add the oats, coconut, sugar, cranberries, and almond flakes and mix. Add the maple syrup to the hot melted butter and mix. Add the butter mixture to the dry ingredients and mix well. Pour the mixture into the baking sheet and press into place with your hands. Bake for about 15 minutes until golden brown. Let cool before slicing. Store in an airtight container for 3 to 4 days or freeze for 2 to 3 months.

CHICKEN AND LENTIL SALAD

SERVES 4

This dish only takes about ten minutes to prepare, and that makes it perfect for busy week-nights. Serve it with some low-FODMAP bread or crackers for a well-balanced meal. You could use two different low-FODMAP vegetables, if you like, but the crunch of the fennel and radish works so well with the tender chicken and lentils.

For the salad

17.6 ounces (500 g) cooked chicken

1 cup (198 g) canned lentils, washed
   and drained

1 fennel bulb, sliced

4 radishes, sliced

2 cups (110 g) salad leaves

½ cup (60 g) toasted chopped walnuts

For the dressing

2 tablespoons (20 g) capers, drained
   and rinsed

Juice of ½ a lemon

3 tablespoons (45 ml) olive oil

3 tablespoons (45 g) plain
   lactose-free yogurt

Mix all the salad ingredients together in a serving bowl. Mix the dressing ingredients in a separate bowl and then drizzle over the salad. Serve immediately. Store leftovers in the fridge for 2 to 3 days.

SPINACH AND CHEESE QUESADILLAS

SERVES 8

This Mexican-inspired vegetarian meal is quick and well-balanced. Go easy on the oil and cheese if fat triggers your symptoms and omit the tomatoes if you have reflux. You can swap the spinach for bok choy or kale or add some ground meat for extra protein. Have half a quesadilla per sitting.

⅔ cup (150 g) cottage cheese

2 cups (60 g) baby spinach leaves

8 large low-FODMAP tortillas

1 cup (164 g) corn kernels, cut from a fresh cob

1 tomato, diced (omit for reflux)

1 spring onion, sliced finely (green part only)

1 teaspoon garlic-infused oil (omit for reflux)

1 tablespoon (15 ml) olive oil

1½ cups (180 g) grated mature cheese

Preheat the broiler in the oven. Place the cottage cheese and spinach in a food processor and process to a paste. Place 4 tortillas on a baking sheet and spread the mixture over the tortillas.

Combine the corn, tomato (if using), and spring onion. Season and spoon onto the tortillas over the spinach mixture. Combine the olive oil and garlic oil (if using) and drizzle over the corn mixture. Top each with another tortilla. Scatter the cheese over the tortillas and drizzle a little more oil over them. Place them in the oven under the broiler until the cheese is bubbling and golden, about 3 to 4 minutes. Serve immediately.

PASTA WITH MEAT SAUCE

SERVES 4

This recipe is based on a classic Italian ragu, and the infusion of flavors is worth the long cooking time. You can omit the bacon, but it does lend the sauce a rich, smoky flavor. Have 1 cup (107 g) of cooked pasta and about ½ cup (112 g) of the meat sauce at a sitting and then use the leftover sauce to fill a pie made with my low-FODMAP pastry (see page 208) for tomorrow's dinner.

WEEK THREE
Dinners

2 tablespoons (30 ml) light olive oil

1 spring onion, finely sliced (green part only)

½ celery stalk, finely chopped

1 carrot, peeled and finely chopped

1 cup (82 g) cubed eggplant

17.6 ounces (500 g) ground beef

4.4 ounces (125 g) bacon, finely chopped

½ cup (117 ml) dry red wine

2½ cups (585 ml) garlic- and onion-free beef stock or chicken stock

2 tablespoons (32 g) tomato paste (omit for reflux)

Salt and pepper

1 cup (235 ml) lactose-free milk

4 cups (580 g) cooked low-FODMAP tagliatelle or fettuccine

Finely grated Parmesan cheese

Heat the oil in a large saucepan over medium-high heat. Add the spring onion, celery, carrot, and eggplant. Sauté until soft, about 8 to 10 minutes. Add the beef and bacon. Sauté, breaking up the meat with the back of a spoon, until browned, about 15 minutes. Add the wine and boil for 1 minute. Add the stock and tomato paste (if using). Stir to combine. Reduce the heat and simmer, stirring occasionally, about 1½ hours. Season with salt and pepper.

Bring the milk to a simmer in a small saucepan and then add to the sauce. Partially cover the saucepan and simmer, stirring occasionally, for about 45 minutes, adding more stock if needed. Or, if there seems to be too much liquid, remove the lid and boil it hard until it reduces. Divide the pasta between 4 bowls, and top each with the meat sauce. Top with grated Parmesan and serve immediately. Store the meat sauce (without the pasta) in the fridge for 2 days or freeze for 2 to 3 months.

TUNA PASTA SALAD WITH SNOW PEAS AND RADISHES

SERVES 4

Packed with tuna and crunchy, low-FODMAP vegetables, this pasta salad is another quick weeknight meal. Substitute salmon or any other canned fish for the tuna or use another type of mature cheese in place of the Brie. You can have up to a quarter of this recipe per serving. Leftovers make great lunches or dinners for the following day.

2 cups (290 g) low-FODMAP pasta

6.5 ounces (185 g) canned tuna (in spring water), broken into chunks

4.4 ounces (125 g) Brie, roughly chopped

½ cup (60 g) roughly chopped walnuts

½ cup (25 g) bean sprouts

2 cups (60 g) baby spinach

5 radishes, roughly chopped

10 snow peas, cut into thirds

2 tablespoons (28 g) garlic- and onion-free mayonnaise

Juice of ½ an orange

1 tablespoon (15 ml) lemon juice

Salt and pepper

1 tablespoon (4 g) finely-chopped fresh oregano

Cook the pasta in boiling water until al dente. Drain and rinse with cold water to cool it down. Place in a serving bowl. Drain the tuna and add it to the bowl, followed by the Brie, walnuts, and vegetables. Combine the mayonnaise with the orange and lemon juices. Mix in the oregano and season to taste. Spoon over the salad, and mix gently to coat all the ingredients. Store leftovers in the fridge for up to 2 days.

LAMB CURRY

SERVES 4

This is a basic curry recipe that you can vary with different meats and low-FODMAP vegetables. Top 1 cup (165 g) of cooked rice with a quarter of this recipe for a single serving. If you have reflux, take care: this curry may be too spicy for you, so try a smaller helping first.

1 tablespoon (15 ml) light olive oil

1 teaspoon ground cumin

2 teaspoons (4 g) ground gingerroot

2 teaspoons (4 g) ground coriander

1 teaspoon ground turmeric

2 cloves

4 cardamom pods

Small cinnamon stick

1 chile, finely chopped (omit for reflux)

2 spring onions, sliced (green parts only)

17.6 ounces (500 g) diced lamb

2 zucchini, sliced

1 carrot, sliced

1 potato, diced

½ cup (117 ml) water

Heat the oil in a saucepan. Add the spices and chile (if using) and cook for 2 minutes to release the flavors. Add the spring onions and cook for 1 minute more. Add the meat and brown well. Add the carrot and potato. Stir to combine and add the water. You may need to add a little more as the curry cooks, so check it regularly. Cover and cook for 1½ hours. Remove the cardamom pods and cinnamon stick and serve hot over rice. Store leftovers in the fridge for 2 days or freeze for 2 to 3 months.

SEAFOOD PIES

SERVES 4

Each of these pies constitutes a complete meal, so there's no need to worry about additional side dishes. You could replace the mixed seafood with smoked fish. You could also use sweet potato for the mashed-potato topping—make sure to eat no more than half a cup (55 g) per serving. You can have up to a quarter of this recipe safely.

WEEK THREE
Dinners

2 large potatoes, peeled and chopped

4 tablespoons (56 g) butter, divided

1 red bell pepper, diced (omit for reflux)

1 zucchini, diced

2 tablespoons (20 g) white rice flour

1 cup (235 ml) lactose-free milk

17.6 ounces (500 g) mixed seafood

Salt and pepper

Grated mature cheese, such as Cheddar

Preheat the oven to 350°F (180°C, or gas mark 4). Boil the potatoes in salted water until tender and then mash them with 2 tablespoons (28 g) of the butter.

Heat a little oil in a skillet. Cook the pepper (if using) and zucchini until tender.

Melt the remaining butter in a large saucepan. Add the flour and stir to combine. Cook for 2 to 3 minutes until well combined. Add the milk a little at a time, stirring well in between additions, to create a thick white sauce. Add the cooked pepper and zucchini. Add the seafood. Season to taste.

Divide the mixture between 4 small casserole dishes or spoon into one larger one. Pile the mashed potatoes on top and scatter the cheese over the potato. Place the pies in the oven for 10 to 15 minutes to brown the tops and melt the cheese. Serve immediately. Store leftovers in the fridge for up to 1 day.

DIARY PAGE | **WEEK THREE** | DATE ___/___/___

SLEEP _____ hours   from _____ to _____

Quality of sleep _____

_____

_____

RELAXATION _____ minutes   from _____ to _____

Type _____

_____

_____

EXERCISE _____ minutes   from _____ to _____

Type _____

_____

_____

BOWEL MOVEMENTS _____ number   times _____

Type* _____

_____

_____

MEDICATION

Type _____

_____

_____

SUPPLEMENTS

Type _____   _____

_____   _____

_____   _____

*To find what type of bowel movement you've had, search the Internet for "Bristol Stool Chart."

FOOD JOURNAL | WEEK THREE

MEAL	TIME	NOTES/SYMPTOMS
Breakfast		
Morning snack		
Lunch		
Afternoon snack		
Dinner		

Lifestyle Exercise:
PHYSICAL ACTIVITY

Exercise is a vital part of a healthy lifestyle and can significantly improve your physical and mental well-being. Here's how:

- When you exercise you burn calories, which helps you manage your weight.

- It combats a variety of problems including heart conditions, stroke, type 2 diabetes, arthritis, high blood pressure, and high cholesterol.

- Exercise stimulates brain chemicals that may leave you feeling happier and more relaxed and may reduce your risk of depression.

- It lowers your risk for colon and breast cancer.

- Regular physical activity can help keep your thinking, learning, and judgment skills sharp as you age.

- Exercise boosts energy and improves your muscle and bone strength by delivering oxygen and nutrients to your tissues and by helping your cardiovascular system to work more efficiently. It can also slow the loss of bone density that comes with age.

- Exercise helps you to fall asleep faster and deepens your sleep.

- It gives you a chance to relax, enjoy nature, or simply engage in activities that make you happy.

Getting sufficient exercise is especially important for people with IBS. Why?

- Exercise increases colonic motility, transit time (that is, the time it takes for matter to pass through the colon), and transitive intestinal gas, thereby reducing the wind in your system that causes bloating.

- During exercise, the bowel typically quiets down because blood is being pumped to other parts of the body. If you exercise regularly and become physically fitter, the bowel may tend to relax even when you're not exercising.

- Exercise helps tackle the psychological origins of stress by triggering the release of endorphins (brain chemicals that improve mood and promote a sense of well-being).

APPROPRIATE EXERCISE

For people with IBS, it's best to minimize impact because this can irritate the internal organs, including the small and large intestines.

SUGGESTED EXERCISE

Try cycling, walking, swimming, yoga, tai chi, Pilates, golf, stretching, and other low-impact activities you enjoy.

Your Exercise This Week:
35 TO 60 MINUTES A DAY OF EXERCISE

Morning
Stretching and strengthening exercises for
15 minutes

Day
a) If you do cardio exercise during the day, continue
doing so for at least 30 minutes, 5 times a week.

b) If you don't do cardio exercise or exercise
sporadically, start with 15 minutes a day of gentle
exercise for 5 days a week and increase gradually
over a month until you reach 30 minutes. Choose
something from the list on the previous page.

Evening
Gentle stretching exercises for 5 to 10 minutes
before bed

Diet Integration: **EATING OUT**
By now, you're used to following a low-FODMAP
eating plan, but what happens when you're eating out, sharing a meal with friends, or going to a
party? Here's how to make sure you stick to your
diet—while having fun, too, of course.

GUESTS FOR DINNER
If you're having a dinner party at your home, then
the sky is (almost) the limit. Any of the recipes in
this book will impress your guests, and they'll never
guess that the menu is low-FODMAP.

EATING AT THE HOME OF FRIENDS
If you are eating at a friend's house, make sure you
contact him or her as soon as you get the invitation.
Mention your main triggers, such as garlic and
onions, if your host doesn't already know about

them. That way, he or she will have time to prepare
his or her menu accordingly.

Suggest bringing some of the food that could
be most troublesome for your host. For instance,
you might offer to bring a low-FODMAP bread
and dessert because many traditional desserts are
off-limits.

FORMAL DINNER PARTIES
This depends on your relationship with the host
or hostess. If you don't know him or her well—for
example, if the host is your boss—you could get
in touch ahead of time and mention a couple of
restrictions, rather than go into an extended explanation of what you can and can't eat. Unfortunately,
there may be occasions when you have to bite the
bullet and eat what's put in front of you if you feel
that the offense given by your rejection might be
greater than your physical pain.

COCKTAIL PARTIES
It can be difficult to keep track of what you're
drinking at cocktail parties, but first and foremost,
you need to limit your alcohol. There's often a
nonalcoholic punch on offer, but that could contain
high-FODMAP fruit and sugar-laden carbonated
drinks, so avoid it. Instead, have a glass of dry wine
or up to 1 ounce (30 ml) of gin with lime juice and
soda and then switch to water to be safe.

A variety of finger foods will probably be passed
around on trays. It is perfectly acceptable to ask the
server for the ingredients of each one so that you
can make wise choices. That way, you won't have to
leave early. As a precaution, eat beforehand to avoid
getting so hungry that you are tempted by the food
at hand, whether it's low-FODMAP or not.

STAYING OVERNIGHT AT SOMEONE ELSE'S HOME

As with dinner parties, let the hostess know in advance that you have specific dietary needs and offer to bring suitable food with you to lessen her load. Most people have oats or some kind of non-wheat-based cereal for breakfast, but if you malabsorb lactose, you may need to bring your own long-life lactose-free milk. Also, keep an array of nonperishable low-FODMAP snacks in your luggage for emergencies.

A SIT DOWN FIXED-MENU MEAL, SUCH AS A WEDDING

On occasions like these, you usually can't phone ahead to order specially made food, but you could certainly try. Eat something before the event and hope that some of the food served will be suitable. Vegetables such as potatoes and carrots should be fine, and the same goes for most meat or fish—just scrape off any added sauce. Take some snacks with you just in case the food is elaborate and you can't tell what is in it.

EATING AT A RESTAURANT

First of all, do your homework in advance: Check out the restaurant menu online. Identify a few suitable possibilities and then phone the restaurant and ask to speak to the chef. Explain your main issues, such as lactose, wheat, garlic, and onions, and see if the two of you can agree on a dish that will keep you safe. That way, when you arrive at the restaurant, you'll be all set—while everyone else is fussing around trying to decide what to eat.

If you have a choice regarding the restaurant, then choose Japanese: it's the cuisine that's most likely to offer a variety of dishes with low-FODMAP ingredients. However, most restaurants will have grilled chicken or fish, which can be served with a mixed plate of suitable vegetables and, perhaps, rice. The simpler your meal is, the better.

In case you find yourself out with friends and you all decide spontaneously to stop and eat at a restaurant, keep a laminated card with you that has a list of your main food issues. Include only triggers that can be hidden in food, such as garlic, onions, wheat, and lactose. Most other nonpermitted foods are in the menu descriptions or are visible on the plate. Show this card to the wait staff and ask them to show it to the chef so he or she can suggest a safe meal. Be sure to ask whether any meat has been marinated in garlic or onions. Tell them you are allergic to the items on the card so that they'll be extra careful. Be clear and confident in your communication with them: If the day is going well, you don't want a setback, so stand up for yourself with the staff. After all, you are paying to eat there, and you don't want a bellyache for your money.

KANE

Kane is a long-distance runner. That means he does extraordinary things—like running across deserts for days on end. He also has IBS with diarrhea, so the lack of trees or bushes in deserts is a privacy problem when attacks strike unexpectedly—which, of course, is par for the course with this disorder. Kane was at rock bottom when he got in touch with me. He had stopped competing, and even his training was in serious jeopardy. In fact, he wasn't venturing very far from his home at all.

Like most sufferers with IBS-D, Kane's symptoms disappeared rapidly on the low-FODMAP diet. Within a week, his voice sounded completely different during our weekly phone calls: he was upbeat and cautiously excited about the future. At that point, he had yet to go through the reintroduction stage of the diet. When he did, he hit a trigger food with his very first test—mango, with which he was testing for fructose. Just half a cup (90 g) laid him

flat on his back in pain. Kane was discouraged—especially after having felt so well at first—and it took some strength for him to pick himself up and continue with the process. But he stuck it out because he recognized that he was making progress and his diet profile was becoming clearer.

And his courage paid off. By the end of the program, Kane and I knew exactly what his major and minor triggers were and which foods didn't cause him any issues, even though they were high-FODMAP. Now, Kane had his diet for a lifetime which would keep him permanently symptom-free. In our final phone call, he was so excited about life that his words tripped over each other, and I just wished I had recorded the conversation! He had returned to his full training program, and he was looking forward to his first long-distance competition in far too long.

The Reintroduction Phase
Incorporating Foods Back Into Your Diet

YOUR REINTRODUCTION PLAN

By now, you should have been symptom-free for a while, and you should be psychologically prepared for the reintroduction stage of the diet. Symptoms will return when you hit on a trigger food or group, and this will take a little fortitude. It's important to view this as part of the process. Every food that triggers your symptoms represents a little more knowledge that you didn't have before.

I recommend that you purchase *The Monash University Low FODMAP Diet* booklet, published by Monash University. You can buy it directly from the university online. It lays out each food and the FODMAP group it contains in a graph form. This will be particularly important when you reach week 6, so order it now.

HOW TO DO THE TESTING

Here's how testing works. You'll test each food in the morning with breakfast, or maybe with your morning tea, so that you can observe the effects during your waking hours. Test the food by consuming only half a serving or "dose" first, so that you don't have a major reaction and put yourself out of action completely for a couple of days. Then, throughout the rest of that day, you have to make sure that there are no other variables in your diet. You must only eat food that you're one hundred percent sure you won't react to—food that you've eaten before during the elimination stage of the diet.

If you react to the half-dose, you wait for at least a couple of days until all your symptoms have disappeared before you try another test. If you don't react to that half-dose, then test yourself the following morning at the full dose. If there is still no reaction, you've gotten the information you need. If you do react to the full dose, you'll have to wait about two days until the symptoms are gone before doing other tests. But now you know that you can eat high-FODMAP foods in that group in small amounts.

These are the foods you'll use to test for each FODMAP group:

- Fructose: ½ cup (90 g) fresh or frozen mango, then 1 cup (180 g) mango

- Lactose: ½ cup (117 ml) milk, then 1 cup (235 ml) milk

- Sorbitol: 5 fresh or frozen blackberries, then 10 blackberries

- Mannitol: ½ cup (50 g) cauliflower, then 1 cup (100 g) cauliflower

- GOS: Test individually

- Fructans: Test individually

Even if you "pass" a group, don't add those foods back into your diet until all the testing is finished, so that your base diet is always the same.

Good luck with the testing! And when you experience a reaction, remember that this is all part of the process. You're working toward creating your ideal diet as an individual. It'll be well worth the temporary pain and discomfort.

Breakfast	2 CHICKEN AND SWISS CHARD FRITTERS (page 122) and 1 cup (210 g) cooked polenta *or* 2 to 4 ounces (60 to 125 g) chicken, 1 cup (36 g) Swiss chard, and 1 cup (210 g) polenta *plus* 1 large or 2 small kiwi fruit *and* weak tea or coffee (optional)
Morning Snack	SWEET POTATO FRIES WITH COTTAGE CHEESE DIP (page 126) *or* ¼ cup (55 g) cottage cheese, up to 20 small rice crackers, and 1 cup (30 g) spinach *plus* 1 cup (235 ml) lactose-free milk
Lunch	Leftover dinner recipe *or* 2 ounces (60 g) tuna, 2 radishes, and 1 cup (107 g) low-FODMAP pasta *plus* 1 cup (150 g) grapes *and* a glass of water
Afternoon Snack	1 CHOCOLATE CHIP AND PEANUT BUTTER COOKIE (page 132), ¾ cup (170 g) lactose-free yogurt, ¼ stalk of celery *or* up to 20 small rice crackers, ¼ stalk of celery, and ¾ cup (170 g) lactose-free yogurt *plus* a glass of water
Dinner	LAMB AND ZUCCHINI KEBABS (page 136), 1 potato *or* 1 lamb filet, ½ cup (60 g) zucchini, 1 potato *plus* a glass of water

Notes:

- While recipes have been suggested for the meal plans, feel free to choose an alternative from this week's recipes or those from the past three weeks.
- Kiwi fruit is particularly indicated if you have constipation since it has a mild laxative effect.
- You can substitute the Swiss chard with any green leafy vegetable, such as spinach or bok choy.

SCRAMBLED EGGS WITH SMOKED SALMON AND SPINACH

SERVES 2

Scrambled eggs take just minutes to make, so they're a quick, protein-rich breakfast (or a lunch or dinner). Here, they get extra protein from smoked salmon and plenty of vitamins from baby spinach. Eat half of this recipe with a starchy vegetable, such as 1 medium potato or ½ cup (66 g) of parsnips, or even a grain like 1 cup (210 g) of cooked polenta or 1 cup (107 g) of cooked low-FODMAP pasta.

4 eggs

¼ cup (58 ml) lactose-free milk

Salt and pepper

1 cup (30 g) finely chopped baby spinach

1.8 ounces (50 g) smoked salmon,
    cut up small

2 teaspoons (9 g) butter

Beat the eggs, milk, and seasoning in a medium bowl until frothy. Add the spinach and salmon and blend through. Heat the butter in a skillet until melted and hot. Add the egg mixture.

As the eggs begin to set, pull the eggs across the skillet with a spatula to form soft curds. Continue cooking in this way until thickened and no visible liquid egg remains. Do not stir constantly. Remove from the heat and serve immediately.

CHICKEN AND SWISS CHARD FRITTERS

SERVES 4

These fritters are a good way to use up any leftover meat and low-FODMAP vegetables. Canned tuna (in spring water, not oil) would be a good substitute for the chicken. Remove as much oil after cooking as possible so that the fat doesn't cause symptoms. They also work well for lunch or dinner: have two fritters alongside 1 cup of cooked rice (165 g) or quinoa (185 g) and 1 medium plantain or ½ cup (168 g) of water chestnuts.

1 zucchini

1 cup (36 g) finely chopped Swiss chard

2 tablespoons (8 g) finely chopped fresh parsley

2 spring onions, finely sliced (green parts only)

1 cup (140 g) chopped cooked chicken

4 eggs

2 tablespoons (20 g) white rice flour

Salt and pepper

2 tablespoons (30 ml) light olive oil

Grate the zucchini and squeeze out all the water thoroughly. Place in a bowl with the chard, parsley, spring onions, and chicken. Lightly beat the eggs, add them to the bowl, and mix together. Add the flour and season well.

Heat the olive oil in a large skillet and drop in 8 spoonfuls of the batter. Flatten to form patties.

Cook on both sides until firm and brown, about 2 to 4 minutes per side. Once cooked, place them on paper towels to absorb the oil. Serve immediately or let cool completely and store in the fridge for 2 to 3 days.

TROPICAL MUESLI

SERVES 12

You might already have tried a muesli recipe in week 2, and the same rules apply to this one. Oats may have too much fiber for you, so test your tolerance levels, especially if you have IBS with diarrhea. On the other hand, oat-rich muesli can be great for people with constipation. Have a little more than ¼ cup (30 g) of this tropical muesli with lactose-free milk and lactose-free yogurt at a sitting.

3 cups (240 g) instant oats

1 cup (85 g) toasted desiccated coconut

1 cup (178 g) dried banana chips

1 cup (160 g) chopped dried papaya

1 cup (120 g) toasted walnuts

½ tablespoon (3 g) turmeric

½ tablespoon (3 g) ground gingerroot

Simply mix all the ingredients together. Store in an airtight container for 2 to 3 weeks.

FETA AND BACON DIP

SERVES 4

Together with low-FODMAP crackers, this rich dip makes a complete snack, but don't over-indulge. You can have the equivalent of ½ cup (125 g) of feta and ½ cup (75 g) of red peppers at a sitting. (If you can, make the dip with preservative-free bacon.) It's perfect as an appetizer, too. Serve it to guests with crackers or chips.

8.8 ounces (250 g) feta cheese

Black pepper

1 tablespoon (1 g) chopped cilantro

½ red bell pepper, roughly chopped
   (omit for reflux)

2 slices of thick bacon, fried and chopped
   into small pieces

Place the feta, black pepper, and cilantro in a small processor and process until smooth. Add the red pepper (if using) and process a little so that the red pepper is more finely chopped, but not pulverized. Transfer the dip to a serving bowl, add the bacon, and fold through. Store in the fridge for 3 to 4 days.

SWEET POTATO FRIES WITH COTTAGE CHEESE DIP

SERVES 4

These sweet potato wedges are great as the starchy element in just about any meal. When they're served with a savory cottage cheese dip or with any of the other dips in this book, they make a delicious snack. They're baked, not fried, and they use less oil than traditional fries, which is safer for people with a lower tolerance for fat. You can have the equivalent of ½ cup (55 g) of sweet potatoes per serving.

For the dip

7 ounces (200 g) of cottage cheese

1 spring onion (green part only)

1 cup (30 g) spinach leaves

1 teaspoon toasted cumin seeds

Salt and pepper

For the potatoes

2 sweet potatoes, peeled

1 tablespoon (14 g) butter, softened

½ teaspoon salt

3 tablespoons (45 ml) light olive oil

1 teaspoon garlic-infused oil
   (omit for reflux)

2 teaspoons (5 g) ground cumin

1 teaspoon dried oregano

½ teaspoon chile powder (omit for reflux)

First, prepare the dip. Combine all the ingredients in a food processer and pulse until smooth. Set aside in the fridge.

Then, prepare the potatoes. Preheat the oven to 350°F (180°C, or gas mark 4). Boil the sweet potatoes until not quite tender. Let cool slightly and then cut lengthwise into strips. Combine the butter with the rest of the ingredients. Coat the strips in the butter mixture and spread on a baking sheet. Bake for 1 hour, turning once. Serve immediately alongside the dip. Store leftover dip in the fridge for 2 to 3 days.

CHICKEN AND PESTO BLINIS

SERVES 8

Whip up these nibbles on the spot to impress guests when they drop in for drinks. Pesto works well here, but feel free to use whatever you have in the fridge to make a variety of toppings. You can also use the blini recipe to make pancakes for dinner and serve them with a protein, such as canned salmon, and ½ cup (75 g) of bell peppers or, if you have reflux, 1 cup (90 g) of cabbage. Or you can serve them for breakfast with a low-FODMAP fruit and lactose-free yogurt.

For the blinis

2.9 ounces (83g) white rice flour

0.8 ounces (21 g) tapioca flour

0.7 ounces (21 g) potato starch

½ teaspoon baking powder

Pinch of salt

1 egg, lightly beaten

½ cup (117 ml) lactose-free milk

For the pesto

2 cups (48 g) basil leaves

1½ tablespoons (14 g) pine nuts

1.4 ounces (40 g) Parmesan cheese

1 teaspoon garlic-infused oil
   (omit for reflux)

Olive oil

Salt

For the toppings

Cooked chicken

Garlic- and onion-free mayonnaise

Paprika

First, prepare the blinis. Sift together the flours, potato starch, baking powder, and salt. Add the egg and mix well. Add the milk slowly, mixing well between additions.

Melt a little butter in a heavy flat-bottomed skillet. Once the butter is sizzling, place spoonfuls of the batter into the skillet. When bubbles form all over the blinis, flip them over and cook them on the other side. Repeat with the rest of the mixture, adding a little more butter to the skillet after each batch.

Then, prepare the pesto. Place the basil, pine nuts, and cheese into a food processor and process until finely chopped. Add the garlic oil (if using) and 1 tablespoon (15 ml) of olive oil at a time until you reach the desired consistency, pulsing between additions. Season with salt to taste.

Spread this pesto sauce onto each blini and top each with a few pieces of cooked chicken, followed by about 1 teaspoon of mayonnaise and a sprinkle of paprika. Serve immediately.

CUSTARD BASKETS

SERVES 3

Don't let extra bread go to waste. Use it in this simple sweet treat. It only uses low-FODMAP kitchen staples, so you can make it anytime. Be sure to crisp up the bread in the oven as a nice counterpoint to the soft custard. Serve with up to 10 raspberries or up to 20 blueberries and a little whipped cream, if you like. Have no more than two baskets per serving.

8 slices of white low-FODMAP bread, crusts removed

Softened butter

¼ cup (30 g) dried cranberries

1½ tablespoons (20 g) white sugar

3.5 ounces (100 ml) lactose-free milk

1 egg

½ teaspoon vanilla extract

Cinnamon

Preheat the oven to 350°F (180°C, or gas mark 4). Butter a 6-capacity mini-loaf pan. Butter both sides of the bread and cut two of the slices into quarters. Press one slice of bread into each of the 6 mini-loaf pans, making sure you cover three sides. Use one of the quarters to fill each of the exposed short sides. Place in the oven and bake for 5 to 10 minutes or until toasted but not burned. Remove from the oven and scatter the cranberries over the bread bases.

Heat the sugar and milk in a small saucepan until almost boiling. Lightly beat the egg with the vanilla and pour it slowly into the milk while stirring vigorously. Heat for 1 minute.

Pour the custard into the bread baskets, taking care not to overfill them. Sprinkle with cinnamon. Cover with aluminum foil and bake for 20 minutes. Let stand for 5 minutes before serving. Serve warm or cold. Store leftovers in the fridge for 2 to 3 days.

PINEAPPLE AND PECAN CAKE

SERVES 12

Extra-moist and studded with nuts and dried cranberries, this pineapple cake is delicious. Be careful not have more than a small slice at a time. If you're making it for a special occasion, you could cover it with a frosting made from powdered sugar, butter, and water. If fructose is a trigger for you, you'll have to reduce the size of your slice.

2 cups (316 g) white rice flour

½ cup (64 g) tapioca flour

½ cup (96 g) potato starch

1 teaspoon baking powder

1 teaspoon ground gingerroot

Pinch of salt

1 cup (200 g) white sugar

½ cup (55 g) chopped pecans

½ cup (60 g) dried cranberries

3 eggs

1 teaspoon vanilla extract

1½ cups (354 ml) light olive oil

1 can (8 ounces, or 225 g) of crushed pineapple

3 just ripe bananas, mashed

Preheat the oven to 350°F (180°C, or gas mark 4). Sift together all the dry ingredients except the sugar. Add the sugar and combine. Then add the pecans and dried cranberries. Lightly beat the eggs with the vanilla. Add the eggs to the dry mixture, along with the rest of the ingredients. Mix until just combined.

Pour the batter into a buttered, floured 9-inch (23 cm) cake pan. Bake for 1 hour. You may need to cover with aluminum foil partway through baking to prevent the top from burning. Remove from the oven and let cool in the pan for 10 minutes. Turn out the cake onto a cooling rack and let cool completely before serving. Store in an airtight container in the fridge for 2 to 3 days or freeze for 2 to 3 months.

CHOCOLATE CHIP AND PEANUT BUTTER COOKIES

MAKES 16 LARGE COOKIES

One cookie is the serving size for these addictive treats, so freeze the rest of the batch to keep them out of temptation's way. Even though they contain sugar, they're considered to be healthy treats because of the other ingredients. It's still important to limit your sugar intake and get as much of it from fresh fruits as possible, so don't have more than one per day.

WEEK FOUR
Sweet Treats

1 cup (80 g) instant oats

¼ cup (24 g) almond meal

¾ cup (64 g) desiccated coconut

1 cup (175 g) chocolate chips

¼ cup (40 g) white rice flour

⅛ cup (16 g) tapioca flour

⅛ cup (24 g) potato starch

¾ teaspoon baking powder

¾ teaspoon baking soda

Pinch of salt

1 cup (260 g) peanut butter

¼ cup (60 ml) light olive oil

½ cup (100 g) white sugar

¼ cup (80 g) maple syrup or golden syrup

2 eggs

1 teaspoon vanilla extract

Preheat the oven to 350°F (180°C, or gas mark 4). Combine the oats, almond meal, coconut, and chocolate chips in a large bowl. Sift the flours, potato starch, baking powder, baking soda, and salt into the oat mixture. Combine the peanut butter, oil, sugar, maple syrup, eggs, and vanilla in a food processor and process to form a smooth mixture. Add the wet ingredients to the dry and blend lightly.

Drop rounded spoonfuls of dough onto a baking sheet lined with parchment paper. Push each round of dough into a circular shape and flatten a little. Bake for 6 minutes or until golden on top. Transfer to a wire cooling rack and let cool until firm. Store in an airtight container for 2 to 3 days or freeze for 2 to 3 months.

CURRY MEATLOAF

SERVES 4

Classic meatloaf is so versatile. You can make it simply, with minimal seasoning; add a handful of fresh herbs; or you can pep it up with lots of spices, as in this recipe. You could also use ground chicken, pork, or lamb instead of the beef. Make sure you keep some for lunch the next day—it's delicious even when it's served cold. Serve with ½ cup (55 g) of sweet potatoes or ¼ cup (39 g) butternut squash and a cup (30 g) of spinach.

1 tablespoon (15 ml) light olive oil

1 teaspoon ground turmeric

1 teaspoon ground cumin

1 teaspoon cumin seeds

1 teaspoon ground coriander

½ leek, chopped finely (green part only)

½ red bell pepper, chopped finely (omit for reflux)

1 stalk of celery, chopped finely

17.6 ounces (500 g) ground beef

1 egg

Salt and pepper

Preheat the oven to 350°F (180°C, or gas mark 4). Heat the oil in a skillet and add the spices. Cook the spices gently for a few minutes to release the aromas. Add the vegetables and cook until soft. Let cool slightly.

In a large bowl, combine the cooked vegetables with the raw meat and egg. Oil a loaf pan and press the meat mixture into it. Place in the preheated oven and bake for about 1 hour. Let the meatloaf stand for 10 minutes before slicing and serving. Store leftovers in the fridge for 2 to 3 days.

KALE AND COTTAGE CHEESE GNOCCHI WITH TOMATO SAUCE

SERVES 4 TO 6

Wholesome and filling, this vegetarian meal covers all of the food groups—no side dishes necessary. Use spinach or bok choy in place of the kale, if you prefer. Just make sure to have no more than a quarter of the gnocchi recipe and two tablespoons (30 g) of the tomato sauce at a sitting. Avoid the sauce if you have reflux.

For the gnocchi

16 ounces (450 g) frozen kale

1.2 ounces (35 g) Parmesan cheese

8.8 ounces (250 g) cottage cheese

1 egg

1 egg yolk

4.2 ounces (120 g) white rice flour

2.8 ounces (80 g) tapioca flour

½ teaspoon nutmeg

Salt and pepper

For the tomato sauce

17.6 ounces (500 g) canned
    tomatoes, chopped

1 teaspoon dried oregano

1 teaspoon garlic-infused oil
    (omit for reflux)

Salt and pepper

First, prepare the gnocchi. Boil the kale until cooked, about 3 to 5 minutes. Drain and squeeze as much water out of the kale as possible and chop it finely. Combine the kale with all the gnocchi ingredients. Adjust the seasoning, if necessary. If the mixture is too wet, add more rice flour. If it is too dry, add a little water. When the consistency is firm enough to form a dough, roll the mixture into small balls, about the size of a Ping-Pong ball.

Boil a couple of large saucepans of salted water. When the water is boiling, divide the gnocchi between the pots and boil gently until they float to the top of the water. This may take as little as 1 minute, so watch the pot constantly. Remove the gnocchi with a slotted spoon and place in a bowl.

To make the sauce, combine all the ingredients in a sauté pan. Cook gently for 15 minutes. Place the gnocchi in the sauce and cook for 3 minutes. Serve with extra grated Parmesan on top. Store leftovers in the fridge for 2 to 3 days.

LAMB AND ZUCCHINI KEBABS

SERVES 4

This is a classic Greek dish called *souvlakia*. Serve the kebabs with mashed potato or sweet potato. If you're not a fan of zucchini, substitute any other low-FODMAP vegetable, such as ½ cup of bell peppers (75 g), fennel (44 g), or eggplant (41 g). You can have up to half a cup (60 g) of zucchini—about one skewer's worth. The amount of lamb is unlimited from a FODMAP perspective, so you may want to make up a meat-only kebab for your second skewer.

2 tablespoons (30 ml) olive oil

Juice of 1 lemon

Salt and pepper

17.6 ounces (500 g) lamb steaks

2 zucchini, sliced into thin rounds

Dried oregano, for garnish

Combine the oil, lemon juice, salt, and pepper in a large bowl. Cut the lamb into small cubes and place in the marinade mixture. Stir and let the meat marinate for about 1 hour.

Preheat the broiler. Remove the meat from the marinade. Thread the meat and zucchini onto metal or soaked wooden skewers, alternating between the two. Place the skewers under the broiler for 15 to 20 minutes, turning halfway through. Once cooked, sprinkle with the oregano and serve immediately.

BAKED SALMON WITH ANCHOVY MAYONNAISE

SERVES 4

Salmon has a high omega-3 content, but it is an oily fish, so it's best to have no more than 2 ounces (60 g) per serving if you're watching your fat intake (or test to find out your tolerance level). For the same reason, you should stick to one tablespoon (14 g) of the anchovy mayo. Serve this recipe with ½ cup (55 g) of sweet potato mash and 1 cup (70 g) of broccoli florets for a well-balanced meal.

For the salmon

8 ounces (240 g) salmon filets, deboned if necessary

Light olive oil

Salt and pepper

For the mayonnaise

1 pasteurized egg yolk

2 teaspoons (10 g) Dijon mustard

Splash of water

4 anchovy filets

6.8 ounces (200 ml) light olive oil

1 tablespoon (15 ml) white vinegar

Preheat the oven to 350°F (180°C, or gas mark 4). Place the salmon on a piece of oiled aluminum foil on an oven tray. Drizzle with olive oil and season with salt and pepper. Bake until cooked through (allowing 4 to 6 minutes per ½-inch [1.25 cm] thickness).

Meanwhile, place the egg yolk, mustard, water, and anchovies in a food processor and process until emulsified. Gradually drizzle in the oil while continuing to process. Add the vinegar, season, and mix again. Serve the salmon with the mayonnaise. Store leftover salmon in the fridge for 1 to 2 days and leftover mayonnaise in the fridge for 2 to 3 days.

TOFU AND POTATO SALAD

SERVES 2

This filling vegetarian dish features baked, herbed tofu alongside a low-FODMAP potato salad. If you're a meat-eater, you can substitute any cooked meat, such as chicken, for the tofu. You might also want to replace the yogurt with garlic- and onion-free mayonnaise, or use other herbs in the potato salad (although dill suits the salad especially well). Eat up to half of this recipe at a sitting.

For the potato salad

2 medium potatoes, peeled, cooked, and cubed

1 cup (82 g) eggplant, cooked and cubed

3 spring onions, chopped (green parts only)

2 tablespoons (8 g) chopped dill

½ cup (117 g) plain lactose-free yogurt or garlic- and onion-free mayonnaise

1 teaspoon mustard

Juice of ½ a lemon

Salt and pepper

For the tofu

3 tablespoons (21 g) polenta or low-FODMAP breadcrumbs

1 teaspoon oregano

Salt and pepper

11 ounces (320 g) plain tofu, sliced thinly

Light olive oil

To serve

Baby spinach

First, prepare the potato salad. Combine the potatoes, eggplant, and spring onions in a medium bowl. Combine the dill, yogurt, mustard, lemon juice, salt, and pepper in a separate bowl and mix well. Coat the potato mixture in the dressing. Set aside.

Then, prepare the tofu. Preheat the oven to 350°F (180°C, or gas mark 4). In a shallow dish, combine the polenta, oregano, and seasoning. Coat the tofu slices in the polenta mixture and place on a baking sheet lined with parchment paper. Drizzle with a little olive oil and bake for 15 to 20 minutes until golden.

To serve, lay some baby spinach leaves on a serving dish and pile the potato salad on top. Serve with the baked tofu. Store leftover potato salad in the fridge for 2 to 3 days.

FISH CAKES WITH TARTAR SAUCE

SERVES 2

For a balanced meal, enjoy half of this recipe for homemade fish cakes with a vegetable like 1 cup of kale (67 g) or spaghetti squash (155 g). For a lower-fat version, place them on a baking sheet and bake at 350°F (180°C, or gas mark 4) for fifteen minutes and then skip the sauce and serve them drizzled with lemon juice instead.

For the fish cakes

8.8 ounces (250 g) firm white fish, roughly chopped

1 large potato, peeled, cooked, and mashed

2 spring onions, sliced finely (green parts only)

2 tablespoons (8 g) chopped parsley

3 teaspoons (15 ml) lemon juice

1 egg

Salt and pepper

2 tablespoons (30 ml) light olive oil

Lemon wedges, for serving

For the tartar sauce

½ cup (117 g) garlic- and onion-free mayonnaise

1 tablespoon (15 g) finely chopped garlic-free pickles (gherkins)

1 tablespoon (10 g) chopped capers

1 teaspoon mustard

Salt and pepper

Place the fish in a food processor. Process until finely chopped, but not until it's a paste. Place the fish into a large bowl and add the rest of the ingredients. Combine well. Form the mixture into 8 patties. Place them on a plate, cover with plastic wrap, and put them in the fridge for at least 30 minutes to firm up.

Heat a little light olive oil in a skillet and add the patties. Cook until well browned on both sides.

To prepare the tartar sauce, simply combine all the ingredients in a small bowl. Season carefully to taste. Serve the tartar sauce alongside the fishcakes and a lemon wedge. Store leftover fish cakes and sauce separately in the fridge for 1 day.

PORK AND CRANBERRY SAUCE SUSHI

SERVES 4

When you're eating sushi at a restaurant, you need to be careful of which fillings you select. You also need to pay attention to how the rice is cooked because it may contain high-fructose corn syrup. If you make your own sushi at home, you can be sure it's safe. This recipe takes a little time and skill, but the result is a nutritious meal that covers all the food groups.

For the sushi

1½ cups (275 g) uncooked sushi rice

2½ cups (587 ml) water

½ teaspoon salt

3 tablespoons (45 ml) sushi vinegar

4 nori sheets

9 ounces (250 g) shredded roast pork

1 cucumber, peeled and cut into sticks

1 carrot, peeled and cut into sticks

Cranberry sauce

To serve

Soy sauce

Pickled gingerroot

Wasabi

Place the rice in a saucepan with the water and salt. Bring to a boil. Cook according to the package directions. Remove the rice from the heat and let stand, covered, for 10 minutes. Stir in the sushi vinegar and let cool, uncovered.

Place a sheet of nori, shiny side down, on a bamboo sushi mat. With wet hands, spread ¼ of the rice over the nori sheet, leaving one edge with a ¾-inch (2 cm) strip free. Lay strips of the roast pork down the center of the rice and arrange the cucumber and carrot sticks over it.

Using the bamboo mat as a guide, roll the sushi away from you to firmly enclose the filling. Wrap the roll in plastic wrap and chill for 30 minutes. Repeat with each nori sheet.

Remove from the fridge, slice widthwise into 1-inch (2.5 cm) pieces, and top with a couple spoonfuls of cranberry sauce. Serve with the soy sauce, pickled ginger, and wasabi. Store leftovers in the fridge for 1 to 2 days.

CHICKEN AND RICE SOUP

SERVES 4

This comforting soup is wonderful on the day it's made, but it's even more delicious the next day because the flavors will have had time to combine and intensify. It's a complete meal in itself, but you could serve it with a slice of homemade low-FODMAP bread or a few crackers.

1 free-range chicken

1 bay leaf

10 black peppercorns

3 crushed cardamom pods

1 carrot, chopped

½ stalk of celery, chopped

3 spring onions, chopped (green parts only)

Salt and pepper

1 cup (180 g) jasmine rice

3 cups (210 g) chopped bok choy

Place the chicken in a large saucepan filled with water and add the bay leaf, peppercorns, cardamom, carrot, celery, spring onions, salt, and pepper. Bring to a boil and simmer for about 1 hour until the meat is falling off the chicken. Remove the chicken and pull the meat apart into small, bite-sized pieces.

Sieve the liquid into a second saucepan and return to the boil. Add the rice. When the rice is 8 minutes away from being fully cooked, remove the peppercorns, bay leaf, and cardamom pods from the cooked vegetables. Then, add the chicken, vegetables, and bok choy to the rice. Let the rice finish cooking, season to taste, and serve. Store leftovers in the fridge for 2 to 3 days or freeze for 2 to 3 months.

DIARY PAGE | **WEEK FOUR** | DATE ___/___/___

SLEEP _____ hours   from _____ to _____

Quality of sleep _____

_____

RELAXATION _____ minutes   from _____ to _____

Type _____

_____

EXERCISE _____ minutes   from _____ to _____

Type _____

_____

TIME FOR SELF _____ minutes   from _____ to _____

Type _____

_____

BOWEL MOVEMENTS _____ number   times _____

Type* _____

_____

MEDICATION

Type _____   _____

_____   _____

SUPPLEMENTS

Type _____   _____

_____   _____

*To find what type of bowel movement you've had, search the Internet for "Bristol Stool Chart."

FOOD JOURNAL | WEEK FOUR

MEAL	TIME	NOTES/SYMPTOMS
Breakfast		
Morning snack		
Lunch		
Afternoon snack		
Dinner		

Lifestyle Exercise:
TIME FOR YOURSELF

When someone asks you how you are, how do you answer?

"I wish I had more time for myself."

"I'm so busy I can't think straight."

"I need more hours in the day."

Do any of these responses sound familiar? Today, most people try to fit too much into their lives and end up feeling burned out: Everyone wants a piece of you, and you are too keen to please. So, you juggle a whole lot of responsibilities, and you have no time for yourself. This makes you feel frustrated, tired, overwhelmed, and out of balance. You are always a few steps behind, feel grumpy, and can't give your best to anyone—let alone yourself.

You have to acknowledge your happiness as your number-one priority, and you need to stand up for it at all costs! So, figure out which activities are eating up your time. How many times a day do you check your email? How many times do you go the supermarket each week, or do separate errands that could be grouped together? Learn to say "no" when you're asked to do things you don't really want to do—things that you don't value or that don't bring you satisfaction. Don't let the "If I don't do it, who will?" mentality trip you up. Ask for help from the people around you. Delegate tasks and expect them to get done.

Stop trying to carve out time for yourself. Instead, *create* the time. You are your first priority. If you don't honor this priority, you won't be fully present for the people in your life.

Your Exercise This Week:
20 OR 30 MINUTES A DAY

- Admit that your happiness is important and acknowledge that creating time for yourself is essential.

- Decide on an activity that makes you happy and fulfilled and that's only about you—something you have always wanted to do but never managed to find time for, such as a dance class, surfing, writing in a journal, collecting butterflies, taking a walk alone, taking a bath, or watching movies by yourself.

- Create a daily ritual and schedule your time for self-care—perhaps in the morning before anyone else is out of bed—and practice that activity for 20 to 30 minutes every day.

Now Go and Play!

Diet Integration: TRAVELING

When asked what they'd do if they had more time or money, most people mention traveling. It seems like the idea of sailing away into the wild blue yonder is heaven to everyone—except for those of us with IBS. We start to get stressed out even before we leave the comfort of our own homes. And what's the worst thing you can do if you have IBS? Stress out, of course. So, let's face the various situations you encounter when traveling one by one and then put some coping strategies into place.

RELAX

First and foremost, deal with that stress by breathing deeply whenever your mind starts going into worse-case-scenario mode. Breathe in deeply and then exhale. Repeat.

YOUR BODY CLOCK

Optimally, the mechanisms in our bodies that regulate sleep, appetite, and bowel movements all function according to an internal rhythm. Travel, particularly across time zones, can throw off your body's clock, contributing to gastrointestinal distress. Make sure you get as much sleep as possible. Keep your meals small and eat them at least three hours apart, just as you would at home.

MOVE

Move about as much as possible, even if it's only walking up and down the plane aisles. When you're in an airport, don't just sit down and wait: go for a brisk walk to get your blood pumping and your muscles and joints moving. Light exercise is essential during enforced idle times, such as plane journeys.

DRINK WATER

Dehydration is a very real risk when traveling, particularly on airplanes. And adequate fluid intake is crucial for good digestive health. Drink plenty of bottled water throughout your trip, especially if you are prone to constipation. Avoid all alcohol and caffeine: In addition to contributing to dehydration, they are gut irritants. Water is your friend.

AVOID BACTERIA

You definitely don't want traveler's diarrhea, so take some precautions:

- Drink only bottled or boiled water.

- Avoid street vendors or other potentially unhygienic food sources.

- Avoid raw or undercooked vegetables and fruits.

- Avoid raw or undercooked meats and seafood.

MEDICATION

As a precaution, take medication with you for a worst-case scenario. Bring Imodium for diarrhea or Milk of Magnesia for constipation—or whatever your doctor has prescribed for these situations.

Here are some more tips for traveling with IBS—by air, land, and sea.

TRAVEL BY AIR

1. When booking, ask for an aisle seat close to the restroom. Check in early at the airport and double-check your seating assignment to make sure you have an aisle seat.

2. When packing, be sure to put all your medical supplies and insurance information in your carry-on bag. Checked luggage does occasionally get lost.

3. Pack extra undergarments, wet wipes, tissues, antibacterial hand wash, and any other items you might need in an emergency in your carry-on bag.

4. Check on your boarding time and plan your last bathroom break accordingly because the boarding process can take a while.

5. Passengers are generally not allowed to get up and move about the cabin of the airplane during taxi, take-off, and landing. Ask a flight attendant what time landing may begin and plan to take your last bathroom break beforehand.

6. Remember to pack a low-FODMAP snack or two just in case none of the available food is suitable. If you are flying to other countries, you will need to bring well-packaged foods, which means you'll have to eat processed foods in this instance. Just plan well in advance to make sure you find food that's safe for you.

7. If you are flying with other people, make a deal with them about sharing the food. That way, you could pick out the low-FODMAP food from all the meals and give your traveling companions the rest.

TRAVEL BY CAR

1. In the days before the journey, stick rigidly to the low-FODMAP diet to ensure that you have a very calm gut at the beginning of the trip.

2. Contact local tourist boards or an auto club—or do an Internet search—to find restrooms on your route.

3. If there are few restrooms on the highway, plan your route on normal roads where you are more likely to find a fast-food restaurant or a hotel that has a restroom.

4. If your destination is in an unfamiliar city, obtain a good map and make a note of areas that may have public restrooms, such as tourist information centers, shopping malls, department stores, hotels, and restaurants.

5. Make sure you have enough medication for the duration of your trip, just in case.

6. Many public restrooms aren't clean or well-stocked. Carry a travel pack containing extra undergarments, trial sizes of toilet seat covers, wet wipes, antibacterial hand wash, extra toilet paper, and anything else you might need. If you have to make a dash for the toilet, you can just grab your pack and be off.

7. When possible, arrange your meal schedule around your trip. If you know that you have to use the toilet about an hour after a meal, leave enough time between your last meal and the start of the trip for that bathroom break.

8. Ensure that your traveling companions know that when you say you need to stop and find a restroom you mean NOW. They can also help you scout for restrooms and help explain if you need to jump to the front of the line.

9. Make sure you find accommodation that includes a small kitchenette so that you can prepare a lot of your own food and pack a lunch and snacks.

10. If you eat in restaurants during the trip, use the same strategies you'd use for eating at a restaurant at home. Show your "Foods I Can't Eat" card to the wait staff. If you are traveling in a foreign country, you may need to make up cards in the foreign language.

WEEK FOUR

TRAVEL BY SHIP

1. You can list dietary needs on the guest reservation form: Write down "low-FODMAP diet" and see what happens. Perhaps the staff will contact you and ask for an explanation—or maybe they'll do their own homework by conducting an Internet search.

2. When you arrive on board, ask to speak to the *maître d'* and check whether your food issues have been taken into account. If not, take this opportunity to make these issues clear. It is safer to eat at the a la carte restaurant where the *maître d'* is present at each meal. Buffet-style meals are more difficult to navigate.

3. Go easy on the wonderful cocktails that are available. Many of them will be high-FODMAP, so investigate the ingredients and then only have one.

4. Book shorter on-shore day excursions so you can eat beforehand and be back on board for your next meal. Eating during the excursion could be a problem because menus are usually set menus.

5. Make sure you have your medication and your emergency pack of toilet paper, wet wipes, and change of clothes with you when you disembark for the excursions. Carry your laminated card with you in the local language in case you need to get a snack on the way.

PATRICIA

When Patricia joined my program, she was depressed and afraid to leave the house because her diarrhea was so out of control. She felt continually tired and hadn't had a job for years. Her day consisted of looking after her husband, two teenage children, and an elderly mother. She walked their Alsatian dog once a day, but had to walk around a short block so that she was constantly near the house in case of an emergency, and the dog was lucky if it got a single circuit around the block before Patricia had to make a mad dash to the toilet.

Patricia dedicated her life to other people and gave little thought to her own needs. But she had a spark of self-care left, and it led her to join my program before she was submerged in misery forever. She followed the low-FODMAP meal plans I created for her and the accompanying instructions to the letter, and she stood strong against any interference from her family. Her diarrhea and bloating stopped within days, and she was amazed and ecstatic at the immediate change.

By the third week of the program, she wrote me a special email thanking me for returning her life to her. She was venturing out farther and farther with the dog—in fact, she had just been out for a whole hour—and she said she had actually felt joy for the first time in years. She was noticing the world around her, and she was enjoying her time for herself without needing to rush to the toilet. She told me that being fearless about going out was such a great feeling; now she was walking with confidence. Over the years, she had noticed her freedom slipping away as she became more and more restricted to the house, and she had suffered from the loss of her ability to be outdoors. The freedom to be mobile again without fear was nothing less than a prayer answered.

The day Patricia sent me that email, she made a firm decision to put her health first and her family second because once she was well and happy, the whole family benefitted. She realized that her ill health had been a heavy burden on both her and her family for far too long. Patricia had finally gotten her priorities straight—to the great advantage of everyone around her.

WEEK FIVE

Persevere
Assessing Your Trigger Foods

Hopefully, you haven't encountered too many triggers during your first week of reintroducing test foods. If you have, remember that it is all part of the process. Without this stage, you'd be on the restrictive elimination stage permanently—and in the long term, that would alter your microbiome and aggravate your symptoms. If you've encountered triggers, you will have felt the stark contrast between being symptom-free and having IBS symptoms, which means you may experience your usual symptoms more acutely. For example, when you have symptoms, you may feel you have more gas than usual.

We've already discussed acceptable toilet habits, so let's talk about flatulence for a moment. Flatulence is passing wind, breaking wind, passing gas, farting—whatever you want to call it. The medical term is flatus, and it happens when the muscles in the intestine and the colon contract, pushing gas down toward the rectum.

Where does this gas come from? From swallowing air; talking while eating; eating too fast and gulping in air in the process; or eating in a stressful situation. It can also come from the foods or drinks that we consume. For example, carbonated drinks contain gas, which enters our digestive systems upon consumption. And you might be surprised to learn that smoothies introduce gas into our systems, too. When you make a smoothie, you nearly double the volume of the initial ingredients and the increase consists of air, which enters your intestine. And the third way is through food which should have been digested in the small intestine, but has passed directly into the bowel to be fermented, causing gas. As we know, that's what happens when someone with IBS eats high-FODMAP trigger foods.

The amount of gas a person passes can vary quite considerably, but the average person passes gas between fifteen and twenty-five times a day.

Research shows that people with IBS do not have more gas or pass more wind than people without it. What this research did discover, though, was that the distribution of that gas in the IBS body is different: the gas tends to pool in pockets in people with IBS, which causes distention and bloating. Plus, given an equal amount of gas in the body, the person without IBS doesn't register it as pain, while individuals with IBS feel it acutely. That's due to the faulty messaging system between the brain and the hypersensitive gut of someone with IBS. So, when it comes to gas, there is really no difference between people with IBS and people without it, except for the distribution of gas and the way in which it's registered as pain.

Be sure to keep filling in your diary pages this week. They are crucial during the testing stage: If you don't keep these records, you won't be able to analyze what happens when you react to a food.

Breakfast	**SALMON AND SPINACH STACKS WITH HOLLANDAISE SAUCE** (page 156) *or* 2 ounces (60 g) smoked salmon, 1 cup (30 g) spinach, and 1 potato *plus* 1 cup (122 g) rhubarb *and* weak tea or coffee (optional)
Morning Snack	**CHEESE AND LEEK MINI-LOAVES** (page 160), 1 cup (72 g) lettuce *or* ½ cup (125 g) feta, up to 20 small rice crackers, and 1 cup (72 g) lettuce *and* 1 cup (235 ml) lactose-free milk
Lunch	Leftover dinner recipe *or* 1 lamb filet, ½ cup (60 g) zucchini, and 1 cup (185 g) cooked quinoa *plus* 1 cup (140 g) papaya *and* a glass of water
Afternoon Snack	1 **CHOCOLATE PEANUT BUTTER TRUFFLE** (page 164), ¾ cup (170 g) lactose-free yogurt, and ½ cup (44 g) fennel *or* up to 20 small rice crackers, ½ cup (44 g) fennel, and ¾ cup (170 g) lactose-free yogurt *and* a glass of water
Dinner	**SPICY CAJUN CHICKEN WITH CORN SALSA** (page 172) *or* 1 chicken breast, ½ cob of corn, ½ cup (55 g) sweet potato *and* a glass of water

Notes:

- While recipes have been suggested for the meal plans, feel free to choose an alternative from this week's recipes or those from the past four weeks.
- If you choose an alternative white fish rather than the salmon for breakfast, then you can have up to 4 ounces (120 g).

EGG CREPE ROLL-UPS

SERVES 4

These egg crepes are simply thin omelets that you can roll up easily, and they're a great way to use up leftover vegetables from last night's dinner. I use green beans and pumpkin here, but you could use a different combination, like 1 cup (140 g) of cucumber and 2 medium cooked and mashed plantains.

For the egg crepes

8 eggs

¼ cup (59 ml) lactose-free milk

1 spring onion, finely chopped
   (green part only)

Salt and pepper

2 teaspoons (9 g) butter

For the filling

1 cup (225 g) mashed pumpkin

4 tablespoons (55 g) cottage cheese

20 green beans, cooked

Salt and pepper

Beat the eggs and milk together. Stir in the spring onion and seasoning.

Heat the butter in a skillet and pour in a quarter of the mixture. Let set and then flip over and brown a little on the other side. Slide the crepe out of the skillet, gently spread 1 tablespoon (about 14 g) of cottage cheese over it, and spoon ¼ cup (59 g) mashed pumpkin over the cottage cheese. Place 5 cooked green beans on top, season, and roll up the crepe. Repeat with the rest of the ingredients. Serve immediately.

SALMON AND SPINACH STACKS WITH HOLLANDAISE SAUCE

SERVES 4

This elegant, satisfying breakfast dish contains all the food groups. It's also quite rich, so be sure to stick to a single stack. If you have a low tolerance for fat or have had your gallbladder removed, it may not be suitable for you, even though it is low-FODMAP. If you make the potato patties thicker, you can create a hash brown, which you could pair with an egg and a vegetable, such as a tomato or, if you have reflux, a cup (72 g) of lettuce.

For the stacks

17.6 ounces (500 g) potatoes, peeled and grated

Salt and pepper

1 to 2 tablespoons (15 to 30 ml) light olive oil

4 cups (120 g) chopped fresh spinach

3.5 ounces (100 g) smoked salmon

For the Hollandaise sauce

1 pasteurized egg yolk

½ tablespoon (8 ml) lemon juice

¼ cup (55 g) salted butter, melted

First, prepare the potatoes. Squeeze out all the liquid from the grated potatoes: the drier, the better. Mix in a little salt and pepper. Heat the oil in a skillet. Place 4 large dollops of the potato mixture in the skillet and flatten to form patties. Cook on both sides until brown, about 10 minutes total. Place the patties on paper towels to drain as much of the oil as possible.

Place a few spoonfuls of water in a saucepan and add the spinach. Heat until the spinach is just wilted. Pile on top of the potato patties and top with slices of the salmon.

Then, prepare the Hollandaise sauce. Place the egg yolk and lemon juice in a small food processor and process to combine. Leaving the food processor running, drizzle in the melted butter until it is all incorporated. Adjust the seasoning, if necessary. Spoon a quarter of the sauce over each patty and serve immediately.

BANANA AND TAHINI RICE PORRIDGE

SERVES 2

This porridge makes a nice change from oatmeal. The tahini adds a dollop of protein to the mix. You can replace it with peanut butter, if you like. Make sure to choose a truly low-FODMAP jam that's low in sugar and contains no apple or dates.

½ cup (30 g) rice flakes

½ cup (117 ml) lactose-free milk

1 tablespoon (15 g) tahini

½ tablespoon (10 g) strawberry jam

½ just ripe banana, sliced

1 tablespoon (15 g) plain
   lactose-free yogurt

Place the rice flakes and milk in a saucepan and bring to a boil. Reduce the heat to low and simmer for 1 to 2 minutes. Remove from the heat and let rest for 1 to 2 minutes to thicken up. Stir in the tahini and jam. Serve topped with the banana and yogurt.

COTTAGE CHEESE AND DUKKAH
WITH FRESH BREAD ROLLS

MAKES 12 ROLLS

These quick low-FODMAP bread rolls take just twenty minutes in the oven. They're wonderful served hot and topped with cottage cheese and homemade dukkah (an Egyptian nut-and-spice mixture). Have one roll with up to 4 tablespoons (55 g) of cottage cheese and a sprinkling of dukkah for a snack and add a vegetable—such as 5 snow peas or 2 radishes—for a complete meal.

For the dukkah

1 cup (145 g) almonds

½ cup (72 g) sesame seeds

1½ tablespoons (8 g) coriander seeds

1½ tablespoons (9 g) cumin seeds

½ tablespoon (3 g) fennel seeds

½ teaspoon black peppercorns

Salt

For the bread rolls

1½ cup (192 g) tapioca flour

1½ cup (237 g) white rice flour

1 teaspoon salt

⅓ cup (78 ml) light olive oil

1 cup (235 ml) water

2 eggs

To serve

Cottage cheese

First, prepare the dukkah. Roast the almonds in the oven at a moderate temperature until they are golden brown. Toast all the other seeds in a dry skillet until golden. Place all the ingredients in a food processor or grinder and process until a coarse mixture is formed. Season with salt to taste. Set aside.

Then, prepare the bread rolls. Preheat the oven to 350°F (180°C, or gas mark 4). Sift the two flours and salt together. Combine the olive oil and water in a small saucepan and bring to a boil. Remove from the heat and add to the flour mixture. Mix thoroughly. Add the eggs and mix to combine.

Knead the dough into a ball while in the bowl. Divide the dough into 12 pieces (about 3 inches [7.5 cm] in diameter each) and form each piece into a bun shape. (They won't change in size once baked.)

Place the rolls on a baking sheet lined with parchment paper and bake for 20 minutes. They will remain pale in color, and they will be crunchy on the outside and a little gooey inside. Do not overcook.

To assemble, slice the hot buns in half, spread each half with up to 2 tablespoons (about 28 g) of cottage cheese, and sprinkle with the dukkah. Serve immediately. Store cooled buns in an airtight container in the fridge for 2 to 3 days and microwave each for about 20 seconds before serving. Store the dukkah in the fridge for up to 4 weeks.

CHEESE AND LEEK MINI-LOAVES

SERVES 8

These three-cheese mini-loaves contain all of the food groups, and they are complete snacks in themselves. You can go ahead and use a gluten-free flour mix in place of the three types of flour—as long as it doesn't contain almond, coconut, or soy flour.

¼ cup (60 ml) light olive oil

¾ cup (75 g) finely chopped leeks (green parts only)

½ cup (79 g) white rice flour

¼ cup (32 g) tapioca flour

¼ cup (48 g) potato starch

1 teaspoon baking powder

½ teaspoon salt

½ teaspoon black pepper

3 eggs

1 cup (230 g) plain lactose-free yogurt

6 ounces (170 g) feta cheese

4.6 ounces (130 g) mozzarella

½ cup (60 g) grated mature cheese, such as Cheddar

2 tablespoons (8 g) finely chopped parsley

Preheat the oven to 350°F (180°C, or gas mark 4). Oil a mini-loaf baking pan. Heat the oil in a skillet and add the leeks. Cook about 2 minutes until softened. Set aside.

Sift the dry ingredients together and lightly beat the eggs. Add the yogurt and eggs to the flour mixture, folding in gently. Do not overmix. Add the leeks, cheeses, and parsley. Mix gently again. Spoon the mixture into the mini-loaf pans. Place in the oven and bake for 15 to 20 minutes. A toothpick or skewer inserted into the loaves to test for doneness will always come out wet because of the cheese, so do take them out of the oven after the time indicated.

Let the loaves stand in the pans for 5 minutes before removing. Serve cold or hot. Store in an airtight container in the fridge for 2 to 3 days. Microwave each for 20 to 30 seconds before eating.

SALMON TORTILLA ROLL-UPS

SERVES 4

Make a batch of these roll-ups on the weekend and then portion them into serving sizes and store them in the fridge so you'll have a healthy snack on hand for a few days. Thanks to their impressive presentation, guests will love them, too. Use tuna if you prefer instead of salmon.

7.4 ounces (210 g) canned salmon

1 tablespoon (15 ml) lemon juice

2 tablespoons (28 g) garlic- and onion-free mayonnaise

2 drops of Tabasco sauce

Salt and pepper

4 low-FODMAP tortillas

1 cup (225 g) cottage cheese

2 spring onions, finely sliced (green parts only)

1 tablespoon (4 g) chopped parsley

½ stalk of celery, finely chopped

1 red bell pepper, finely chopped (omit for reflux)

½ cup (17 g) alfalfa sprouts

Combine the salmon, lemon juice, mayonnaise, and Tabasco sauce in a bowl. Season to taste with salt and pepper. Divide the mixture equally between the 4 tortillas and spread it over them from edge to edge.

Combine the cottage cheese, spring onions, and parsley. Season to taste. Spoon a quarter of the mixture over the salmon on each tortilla. Sprinkle the celery, bell pepper (if using), and alfalfa sprouts over the cottage cheese. Don't overload them.

Roll each tortilla up tightly and then roll each in plastic wrap to keep them firmly closed. Place in the fridge for several hours.

Once they are well chilled, remove the plastic wrap, cut them into equal-sized slices, and arrange on a serving plate.

RHUBARB AND HAZELNUT CRUMBLE CAKE

SERVES 12

Rhubarb lends this soft, moist cake a delightful tang, and the hazelnut topping adds a lovely crunch. Serve it to guests alongside coffee or tea; they'll never guess that it's low-FODMAP. Have only a small slice. On special occasions, you can top it with a little whipped cream or lactose-free yogurt.

For the cake

4 ounces (120 g) butter, softened

1½ cups (340 g) brown sugar

1 egg

1⅓ cups (210 g) white rice flour

⅓ cup (42 g) tapioca flour

⅓ cup (64 g) potato starch

1 teaspoon baking soda

Pinch of salt

1 cup (230 g) plain lactose-free yogurt

2½ cups (305 g) chopped rhubarb

For the topping

½ cup (100 g) white sugar

1 tablespoon (14 g) butter

½ cup (58 g) chopped hazelnuts

1 teaspoon ground allspice

Preheat the oven to 350°F (180°C, or gas mark 4). Butter and line an 8-inch (20 cm) springform cake pan.

Beat the butter and sugar together until light and fluffy. Add the egg while beating. Sift the flours, potato starch, baking soda, and salt together. Gradually add the dry ingredients to the butter mixture, alternating with spoonfuls of the yogurt. Fold in gently. Add the chopped rhubarb and mix gently.

Pour the batter into the pan. Mix all the topping ingredients together and sprinkle over the top of the cake. Place in the oven and bake for 40 minutes or until a toothpick or skewer inserted into the center comes out clean. After about 10 minutes of baking, you may need to cover the cake with aluminum foil to keep the top from burning.

Let cool for 10 minutes and then release the springform base and ease the cake out onto a serving plate. Slice and serve. Store in an airtight container for up to 2 days or freeze for 2 to 3 months.

CHOCOLATE PEANUT BUTTER TRUFFLES

MAKES 10 TRUFFLES

These chocolaty, no-cook truffles are special treats, and they're quite rich, so have only one at a time. If you're not a fan of walnuts, replace them with pecans. If the mixture is too sticky to handle, refrigerate it for half an hour to let it firm up before rolling it into balls.

2 cups (160 g) instant oats

⅔ cup (164 g) smooth peanut butter

½ cup (160 g) maple syrup

1 teaspoon vanilla extract

½ cup (60 g) dried cranberries

½ cup (60 g) chopped walnuts

½ cup (87 g) chopped dark chocolate

1 tablespoon (about 5 g) sifted cocoa powder

1 tablespoon (7 g) sifted confectioners' sugar

½ cup (42 g) shredded coconut

Combine all the ingredients in a large bowl. Roll the mixture into 10 small balls. Store in the fridge for up to 3 to 4 days.

LAMB BURGERS

SERVES 4

Have just one of these juicy lamb burgers to stay within safe FODMAP limits. You can add a few more salad leaves on the side, if you like (up to a total of one cup or 55 g). If you have reflux, skip the tomato and replace it with extra sprouts. And it's best not to salt the ground lamb until the patties are cooked: they'll leak out liquid and you'll get a broiled burger instead of a grilled one.

For the burgers

14 ounces (400 g) ground lamb

1 teaspoon ground gingerroot

¼ teaspoon black pepper

Salt

For the sauce

2 tablespoons (28 g) garlic- and
 onion-free mayonnaise

2 tablespoons (10 g) grated
 Parmesan cheese

1 heaped tablespoon (7 g) finely
 chopped mint

To serve

4 low-FODMAP burger buns

4 large slices of tomato (omit for reflux)

Alfalfa sprouts

Salad leaves

Preheat the broiler. Place the lamb in a bowl and combine with the ginger and black pepper. Form the mixture into 4 patties. Place on a grill pan on top of the stove until cooked through (160°F or 71 °C), turning once. Sprinkle with salt.

Combine the mayonnaise, Parmesan, and mint to form a sauce.

Split open the buns and arrange on a baking sheet. Place in the oven until lightly toasted. Remove and spread ½ of a tablespoon (7 g) of the sauce on the bottom half of each bun. Top with the patties, then the tomato slices (if using). Add about 1 tablespoon (2 g) of sprouts to each and finish with a few salad leaves. Top with the remaining bun halves and serve immediately.

BACON, CHEESE, AND LEEK RISOTTO

SERVES 4

This rich risotto makes such a comforting meal, especially on cold winter nights, and it's surprisingly easy to make. You can buy low-FODMAP vegetable and chicken stock in some supermarkets and on the Internet.

2 tablespoons (30 ml) light olive oil

2 cups (200 g) chopped leeks
  (green parts only)

1⅓ cups (240 g) short grain rice

Up to 8 cups (2 L) hot garlic- and
  onion-free chicken or vegetable stock

4 slices of bacon

1 cup (120 g) grated mature cheese

1 cup (40 g) chopped fresh basil

Salt and pepper

Basil leaves, whole, for garnish

Heat the oil in a skillet and add the leeks. Sauté until soft but not burned. Add the rice and stir for 2 minutes to coat all the rice grains with oil and toast them lightly. Add the hot stock gradually, waiting for each addition to be absorbed before adding more. You may not need the full amount of stock.

Heat a little oil in a separate skillet and cook the bacon. Chop into chunks when cooked.

When the rice is almost cooked through, add the bacon, cheese, and basil. Stir until the cheese is melted. Season with salt and pepper to taste, garnish with basil leaves, and serve piping hot.

PARMESAN, TOMATO, AND EGGPLANT "LASAGNE"

SERVES 6

For both health and environmental reasons, it's a good idea to eat vegetarian at least once a week. Try this pasta-free take on vegetarian lasagne: it's meat-free but contains cheese and egg, so it still takes care of your protein needs. (If you have reflux, however, you may want to avoid this recipe because of the tomato.) Have one-sixth of this recipe to stay within safe FODMAP limits.

WEEK FIVE
Dinners

1 medium eggplant

1 cup (250 g) tomato puree, divided

1 cup (100 g) grated Parmesan cheese, divided

6 boiled eggs, sliced

1 cup (120 g) grated mature cheese such as Cheddar, divided

Salt and pepper

Preheat the oven to 350°F (180°C, or gas mark 4). Oil an 8-inch (20 cm) square baking dish. Slice the eggplant into 9 thin slices. Place 3 slices of eggplant in the base of the baking dish. Pour ½ cup (125 g) of the tomato puree over top. Season with salt and pepper and sprinkle with ⅓ cup (33 g) of the Parmesan. Layer the slices of one of the eggs on top. Sprinkle with ½ cup (60 g) of the mature cheese. Repeat these layers once and then finish with a layer of eggplant and eggs. Sprinkle the rest of the Parmesan on top. Season with salt and pepper.

Place in the oven and cook for about 30 minutes until the eggplant is cooked through. Cover with aluminum foil if the cheese starts to burn. Remove from the oven and serve immediately. Store leftovers in the fridge for 1 to 2 days.

MOUSSAKA

SERVES 6

Moussaka is another classic Greek dish. Its fat content can be fairly high, so use very lean ground beef or lamb to stay safe. For a balanced meal, serve it with a medium potato or 1 cup (165 g) of cooked rice. This recipe serves up to six people, and you should have about a sixth of it. Avoid this recipe altogether if you have reflux.

For the ground meat

1 teaspoon ground cumin

1 teaspoon ground turmeric

2 small green chiles, chopped

3 spring onions, sliced (green parts only)

1 teaspoon garlic-infused oil

1 tablespoon (15 ml) light olive oil

17.6 ounces (500 g) lean ground beef or lamb

1 can (14 ounces, or 400 g) of chopped tomatoes

2 tablespoons (32 g) tomato paste

½ cup (117 ml) garlic- and onion-free stock

2 tablespoons (2 g) chopped fresh cilantro

For the cheese sauce

2.6 ounces (75 g) butter

¼ cup (40 g) white rice flour

1½ cups (352 ml) lactose-free milk

1 egg

1 cup (120 g) grated mature cheese

To assemble

2 eggplants

2 tablespoons (10 g) Parmesan cheese

Prepare the ground meat. In a skillet, cook the cumin, turmeric, chiles, and spring onions in the two oils for 2 minutes. Add the meat and brown well. Then, add the tomatoes, tomato paste, stock, and cilantro. Cover and cook for 30 minutes. Set aside.

Meanwhile, prepare the cheese sauce. Melt the butter in a saucepan, add the flour, and cook until it comes together like a dough. Add the milk, a little at a time, mixing to blend in between additions. Add the egg and cheese and stir to melt. Remove from the heat.

Slice the eggplants into thin rounds and place on a baking sheet. Brush with oil and place under a broiler for a few minutes until browned.

To assemble the moussaka, preheat the oven to 350°F (180°C, or gas mark 4). Oil a 12- x 9-inch (30 x 23 cm) baking dish. Place a layer of eggplant slices in the bottom of the dish. Spread half of the meat over the eggplant. Top with another layer of eggplant slices, followed by the rest of the meat. Cover with the last of the eggplant slices. Pour the cheese sauce over top, sprinkle with the Parmesan, and bake for 20 minutes until the top is lightly browned and the moussaka is heated through. Serve immediately. Store leftovers in the fridge for 2 to 3 days.

SPICY CAJUN CHICKEN WITH CORN SALSA

SERVES 4

When it's served with mashed sweet potatoes or potatoes, this simple-yet-flavorful chicken recipe is a complete meal. If you need to keep your fat levels low, bake the chicken and bacon in the oven instead of frying them. Skip the tomatoes and chile if you have reflux. Keep some leftovers for tomorrow's lunch; it'll be just as good on the second day.

WEEK FIVE
Dinners

For the Cajun seasoning

2 teaspoons (5 g) ground cumin

2 teaspoons (4 g) ground coriander

2 teaspoons (5 g) paprika

½ teaspoon salt

1 teaspoon dried oregano

1 teaspoon ground cardamom

For the salsa

6 ounces (172 g) fresh corn kernels

2 tablespoons (2 g) roughly
　　chopped cilantro

1 red chile, finely chopped (omit for reflux)

1 spring onion, finely chopped
　　(green part only)

2 ripe tomatoes, diced (omit for reflux)

1 lemon

1 tablespoon (15 ml) olive oil

Salt and pepper

For the chicken

4 chicken breasts

1 tablespoon (about 7 g) Cajun seasoning

1 tablespoon (7 g) low-FODMAP
　　breadcrumbs

1 to 2 tablespoons (15 to 30 ml) light
　　olive oil

3 slices of bacon

1.8 ounces (50 g) feta, crumbled

To make the seasoning, combine all the ingredients in a small bowl and set aside.

Prepare the salsa. Place the corn, cilantro, chile (if using), spring onion, and tomatoes (if using) in a bowl. Squeeze in the lemon juice and add the oil. Season with salt and pepper to taste. Mix well and set aside.

Cover the chicken with waxed paper and bash it with a rolling pin to flatten it out. Mix the Cajun seasoning and low-FODMAP breadcrumbs together and coat the chicken in it. Heat the olive oil in a skillet and cook the chicken, turning after 3 to 4 minutes, depending on the thickness of the filet, until golden and cooked through. Cook the bacon in another skillet until crispy.

Place the chicken on serving plates. Slice up the bacon and sprinkle it, along with the feta, over the chicken. Serve immediately with the salsa and a ½ cup (55 g) side of mashed sweet potatoes.

TUNA STUFFED PEPPERS

SERVES 4

You and your guests will love this recipe's vivid colors, flavors, and textures. Stick to half a pepper to stay within safe FODMAP limits and add a starchy vegetable, such as 1 cup (133 g) of turnips, or a cup (107 g) of cooked low-FODMAP pasta to make this a complete meal. If you like your peppers al dente, don't prebake them; fill them raw instead. The filling will warm through and the cheese will melt, but the peppers will still be slightly crunchy. Avoid this recipe if you have reflux.

2 bell peppers of any color

1 slice of low-FODMAP bread

1 tablespoon (15 ml) lactose-free milk

6.5 ounces (185 g) canned, drained tuna (in spring water)

1 cup (115 g) shredded mozzarella

1 tablespoon (3 g) finely chopped fresh basil

1 tablespoon (4 g) finely chopped fresh parsley

½ zucchini, chopped finely

1 tomato, deseeded and chopped finely

Salt and pepper

Preheat the oven to 350°F (180°C, or gas mark 4). Cut the peppers in half lengthwise and remove the seeds. Place on a baking sheet and bake for 20 minutes until softened. Remove from the oven and sprinkle with salt.

Soak the bread in the milk to soften it. Place all the remaining ingredients in a bowl and add the softened bread. Mix well to break up and incorporate the bread. Pile the filling into the pepper halves and drizzle each with a little olive oil. Place in the oven for 10 to 15 minutes to heat through and melt the cheese. Serve hot.

LEFTOVER SOUP

SERVES 10

This soup is an ingenious way to use up the leftover vegetables and vegetable stalks you usually throw away. And it'll be different every time you make it because your leftover low-FODMAP vegetables will vary. You can switch up the spices and herbs as long as the flavors blend together well. Have no more than one bowl, or you'll overload on vegetables and exceed your FODMAP limits.

For the stock

1 bok choy leaf and stalk

1 cup (100 g) roughly chopped leeks (green parts only)

Stalk of a small head of broccoli

6 leaves of kale

1 stalk of celery

2 star anise

6 cardamom pods

10 black peppercorns

1 teaspoon cumin seeds

1 tablespoon (2 g) fresh thyme leaves

2 tablespoons (8 g) chopped fresh parsley

2 bay leaves

Sea salt

1 turkey neck

For the soup

10 kale leaves

1 small head of broccoli

1 bunch of bok choy

1 cup (100 g) finely chopped leeks (green parts only)

1 stalk of celery

1 carrot

1 red chile (omit for reflux)

1 tablespoon (2 g) fresh rosemary

1 tablespoon (2 g) fresh thyme leaves

1 small bunch of parsley

Salt and pepper

1 cup (170 g) quinoa

First, make the stock. Roughly chop the first lot of the bok choy, leeks, broccoli, kale, and celery. Place them in a large saucepan with the star anise, cardamom, peppercorns (if using), cumin seeds, thyme, parsley, bay leaves, salt, and the turkey neck. Cover the mixture with water by about 2 inches (5 cm). Boil for 1 hour, occasionally mashing the ingredients with a potato masher. Sieve the mixture and reserve the liquid. Discard the solids: they will contain bone fragments. Transfer the stock back to the saucepan.

Chop up the remaining vegetables and herbs fairly finely. Place all of them into the stock and boil until the vegetables are soft. Add water if the mixture looks too thick.

Transfer the mixture to a large food processor and blend to a smooth soup. Return the soup to the saucepan, add the quinoa, and cook until the quinoa is soft. Adjust the seasoning, if necessary, and serve hot. Store the cooled soup in the fridge for 1 to 2 days.

DIARY PAGE | WEEK FIVE | DATE ___/___/___

SLEEP _____ hours   from _____ to _____

Quality of sleep _____

_____

RELAXATION _____ minutes   from _____ to _____

Type _____

_____

EXERCISE _____ minutes   from _____ to _____

Type _____

_____

TIME FOR SELF _____ minutes   from _____ to _____

Type _____

_____

FAMILY TIME _____ minutes   from _____ to _____

Type _____

_____

BOWEL MOVEMENTS _____ number   times _____

Type* _____

_____

MEDICATION

Type _____

_____

SUPPLEMENTS

Type _____

*To find what type of bowel movement you've had, search the Internet for "Bristol Stool Chart."

FOOD JOURNAL | WEEK FIVE

MEAL	TIME	NOTES/SYMPTOMS
Breakfast		
Morning snack		
Lunch		
Afternoon snack		
Dinner		

Lifestyle Exercise:
FAMILY TIME

These days, as we pursue the material gods, the desire for more and more money eats up our time. And that leaves us with little time for each other. Amassing money and maintaining possessions is exhausting, and it distracts us from what really matters in life: family.

It's important not to take your partner and children for granted. After all, they won't necessarily always be there for you. Spouses may leave if they find someone who values and listens to them; children grow up and fly the nest, taking with them the lessons they've learned about not spending time with family. It's easy to become distant or estranged. So, take action now while your family is intact. You don't have to focus on spending "quality time" with them; you just need to spend time with them, period. Quantity is as important as quality.

HOW CHILDREN LEARN

If you have children, they learn if they matter in this world through whether or not you spend time with them. And the way in which you interact with them is as important as the time you spend with them. Make special moments out of all the routine parts of the day—like helping them dress, bathing them, reading to them at night, and helping them with their homework.

Much of a child's basic learning takes place in the many informal situations that occur in daily family life. Children learn from us. If we always have one eye on the clock and an ear pressed to our cell phones, they will learn that that is how life should be conducted—with half of their focus on something else.

LOVE YOUR PARTNER

If you have a partner, how much time do you spend together actively engaged in each other with no interruptions like TV, phones, computers, and kids? Probably very little. It is very easy for couples to grow apart and live parallel lives which seldom connect. Love needs to be nurtured. Plus, children learn to bring balance to their lives when they see their parents setting aside time for each other and for what truly matters. So, each week, go out on a date for just the two of you—no children or friends allowed.

IDEAS FOR SPENDING TIME WITH CHILDREN

- Make a special family breakfast together on Sundays.

- Instead of splitting up and sharing out the chores, how about tackling them together as a team? For instance, you all clean up one bedroom as a group; then, you move on to the next one together. Work seems a lot less like "work" if you have companions to chatter with! Don't chase the children away because you are so busy with household chores: Include them when they are small and soon they will be competent helpers.

- Choose a movie together and then make popcorn, settle down on the couch, and watch it together.

- Do art projects. They may be messy, but it's a great chance to talk and to learn about what is happening in a child's life.

- Get involved in sporting activities together—such as fishing, watching a football game, roller-blading, or playing with a ball in the backyard.

- Have regular game nights—with no TV and phones turned off.

- Engage in outdoor activities, such as hiking, walking, bicycling, going for picnics, or camping.

And remember that even activities like buying a new pair of shoes or singing songs in the car on the way to school will be great learning moments for the kids—as long as you participate and are truly present in those moments. Remember, you are teaching them that you care and that they matter.

IDEAS FOR YOUR DATE WITH YOUR PARTNER

- Have a restaurant night in which you start with cocktails at one restaurant and have a main meal at another before finishing up with dessert at your favorite chocolate spot.

- Pack a lunch on a Saturday and go for a hike in the nearest national park.

- Splurge on a romantic moonlight dinner cruise.

- Make a backyard picnic with wine, candlelight, and gourmet food.

- Learn a new activity together: try dancing, tennis, or photography.

- Be adventurous and go tandem parachuting, bungee jumping, or rock-climbing.

- Play Monopoly, Pictionary, or cards.

- Go to an amusement park and ride the rollercoaster together.

Your Exercise This Week:
ONCE A WEEK

Families with children:
- Block out weekly family time for participating in one of the previous suggestions—or any other idea you all agree upon.

- Write it into your and your partner's schedules. It cannot be changed or moved.

- Dedicate that period of time solely to the family. Turn your phones off.

Partners:
- Plan a date night for a special activity that you both choose or try one of the ideas on this page.

- Write it into your and your partner's schedules. It cannot be changed or moved.

- Dedicate that period of time solely to your partner. Turn your phones off.

ONCE A MONTH

Families with children:
- Make a date with each child once a month.

- Write it in your schedule. It cannot be changed or moved.

- Discuss in advance what that date is going to entail.

- Dedicate that period of time solely to that child. No cell phones allowed.

Diet Integration:
DEALING WITH FAMILY

Families are built on routine, and most families aren't great when it comes to change. That's how we bring up our children—with fixed mealtimes and bedtimes, regimented so that they learn discipline. Then, you come along with this low-FODMAP bombshell and disrupt some of that routine. So, it's best to sit them down for a formal chat to explain the changes this diet will entail and to set up a few ground rules. Then, schedule weekly meetings so you can give an update on how you're doing and hear how they are coping.

COOKING ONE MEAL FOR THE FAMILY

Your family can eat your low-FODMAP meals at dinner and eat high-FODMAP at the other meals. Low-FODMAP meals can be delicious—and working around low-FODMAP ingredients means less work than you might imagine. For instance, if your kids don't like low-FODMAP pasta, then boil two saucepans of water: one for your pasta and one for theirs. Or buy low-FODMAP buns for your hamburger and use regular wheat buns for theirs.

RESISTING TEMPTATIONS

At first, make sure your ground rules include not waving creamy, sugary cakes or ice cream under your nose. You might be able to ease up on that over time as you build the willpower to resist—because the reward is greater than the pain of erring.

NEGATIVE FAMILY MEMBERS WHO DON'T BELIEVE IN ALLERGIES OR INTOLERANCES

Because IBS is such a silent disorder and because you don't talk about it, this might seem like a flight of fancy to them. You will have to be quietly insistent on sticking to your diet or be prepared to suffer whenever you visit such family members. A clear explanation of the mechanics of what is happening in your body might help sway them. If not, you will have to put up with their doubts, comments, hurt feelings, and attempts to get you to eat forbidden foods. Each family has different dynamics, and you are the best judge of how to handle this.

FAMILY GET-TOGETHERS AND HOLIDAYS

If you are all contributing food to a family event, you can make sure that your offering suits your diet and that it constitutes a well-rounded meal by itself. For example, if you were to take a low-FODMAP chicken pasta salad, for example, then you wouldn't have to eat anything else. But there are sure to be some family members who are supportive and on board with your diet. Coordinate with them to ensure that you have a few dishes to choose from.

CASE STUDY

JESSICA

As a wife and mother of three small children, all of whom had food sensitivities, Jessica was totally overwhelmed. She'd developed IBS after the birth of her third child, and she had never gotten back on her feet again. She had irregular bowel movements which switched back and forth between endless bouts of diarrhea and days of constipation, plus perpetual bloating and explosive gas. She felt ashamed and defeated.

After two years of suffering, she contacted me for help finding a diet that would keep her symptom-free and give her back her previous zest for life: She could hardly recognize the depressed, lackluster creature she had become. Many women in her position soldier on, believing that they have to put their children first, but Jessica was aware of the effect her health was having on her family, and she didn't want her children to grow up with a miserable, grumpy mother. So, she decided to take action.

Initially, it was hard for Jessica to implement the new meal plans I created for her and to take her children's food needs into account, but she persevered, and by the second week, she had regular bowel movements with no bloating. She had also developed a new routine in which her entire family ate the same meals with a few small low-FODMAP-friendly changes. At first, Jessica's family had resisted the changes, but soon they saw how much better her symptoms were as a result, and they adapted to the change in diet with its reduction in processed foods.

She was so relieved when her energy returned and her dark mood lifted. In the third week, she burst into tears when her husband told her that she was a completely different person. The full effect of her IBS on family life really hit her, and she vowed never to look back and to stick to the expanded diet we created for her through the reintroduction stage. Even though she has to be careful, especially when eating out, Jessica is so grateful for her new life, and she can't believe how much it contrasts with the dark, miserable place she had been in for so long.

Expansion
Creating Your Own Low-FODMAP Diet Profile

Congratulations! You've made it to the last week of the program. At this point, you'll probably only have the oligosaccharides left to test. Oligosaccharides are poorly absorbed by the general population, but people without IBS experience little more than a bit of flatulence while people with IBS suffer from gas, bloating, pain, and altered bowel movements if they eat a trigger food. The only way to work out which foods in this list cause you symptoms and which don't is to test them individually.

If you ordered *The Monash University Low FODMAP Diet* booklet in week 4, turn to the section with the heading "Which foods contain poorly absorbed FODMAPs?" Turn to the vegetables list in this section. If a food in the oligosaccharides column also contains a FODMAP group that you have already reacted to in previous testing, then that immediately excludes it. Go through the rest of the list. Decide which foods you would like to test and

ignore the rest. Repeat this with the lists of fruits, legumes and pulses, nuts, and cereals and grains.

Now, work your way through your list, testing each food individually. Use the same rules you followed in chapter 4, testing the food in the morning and keeping the rest of the food you consume that day compliant with a clean elimination diet.

Perform two tests per food with the amounts you consume based on the information given in the lists. For example, if the list says that 1 cup (107 g) of cooked wheat pasta is high in fructans, then test half a cup (54 g) first. Then, if you "pass" that, test the full cup (107 g). If you pass the half-cup (54 g) test but not the full cup (107 g), you know you can include some wheat in your diet in limited amounts. If you pass both tests, you can try having a larger amount—but remember, we do need to keep our meal sizes smalll.

Breakfast	PIZZA POTATO OMELET (page 186) *or* 2 eggs, ½ cup (60 g) zucchini, and 1 potato *plus* 1 cup (150 g) grapes *and* weak tea or coffee (optional)
Morning Snack	PESTO AND PROSCIUTTO BRUSCHETTA (page 190) *or* 1 to 2 ounces (30 to 60 g) prosciutto, up to 20 small rice crackers, and ½ cup (90 g) tomato *and* 1 cup (235 ml) lactose-free milk
Lunch	Leftover dinner recipe *or* 1 chicken breast, ½ cob of corn, and ½ cup (55 g) sweet potato *plus* 1 cup (165 g) pineapple *and* a glass of water
Afternoon Snack	1 slice of BANANA, KIWI, AND COCONUT LOAF (page 196), ¾ cup (170 g) lactose-free yogurt, ½ cup (17 g) alfalfa sprouts *or* up to 20 small rice crackers, ½ cup (17 g) alfalfa sprouts, and ¾ cup (170 g) lactose-free yogurt *plus* a glass of water
Dinner	SHRIMP AND KALE POLENTA (page 202) *or* 4.4 ounces (125 g) shrimp, 1 cup (67 g) kale, and 1 cup (210 g) cooked polenta *plus* a glass of water

Notes:

- While recipes have been suggested for the meal plans, feel free to choose an alternative from this week's recipes or those from the past five weeks.
- Try to find prosciutto which contains no preservatives since additives can be gut irritants.
- If you have reflux, swap out the tomato for 5 snow peas and have 10 strawberries instead of the pineapple.

PIZZA POTATO OMELET

SERVES 4

Omelets are simple, nutritious breakfasts that can cover all the food groups. They're also ideal for using up leftover vegetables from the night before. This vegetarian omelet can do double-duty as a dinner on a busy weeknight because it can be thrown together so quickly.

8 eggs

8 tablespoons (112 ml) lactose-free milk

Salt and pepper

½ tablespoon (7 g) butter

1 large potato, boiled and sliced

1 zucchini, sliced

1 tomato, sliced (omit for reflux)

1 tablespoon (3 g) finely chopped basil, plus more for serving

1 cup (120 g) grated mature cheese

Preheat the broiler. Beat the eggs, milk, and seasoning together. Melt the butter in a large, ovenproof skillet. Add the egg mixture and cook, pulling in the edges to allow the raw egg to fill the spaces, until the base is semi-set.

Evenly distribute the potato, zucchini, and tomato (if using) over the egg mixture. Sprinkle the basil over the top. Cover the whole omelet with the grated cheese. Place the skillet under the broiler on the middle shelf until the cheese is melted. Garnish with fresh basil and serve hot, straight from the skillet.

TUNA AND CARROT FRITTERS

SERVES 3 TO 4

Prepare the batter for these healthy fritters the night before and then cook these up the following morning for a breakfast that covers all the food groups. Or make a batch for dinner and have the leftovers for breakfast. You could substitute zucchini for the carrots, if you squeeze out all the liquid first.

¾ cup (120 g) white rice flour

¼ cup (32 g) tapioca flour

2 teaspoons (9 g) baking powder

¼ cup (30 g) low-FODMAP breadcrumbs

½ teaspoon salt

½ teaspoon black pepper

2 eggs

½ cup (117 ml) lactose-free milk

1 cup (100 g) grated carrot

½ stalk of celery, finely chopped

1 cup (154 g) drained, canned tuna

2 teaspoons (10 ml) lemon juice

2 tablespoons (30 ml) light olive oil

Lemons for serving

Combine the flours, baking powder, breadcrumbs, and seasoning in a bowl. Beat the eggs and milk together in a separate bowl. Stir the egg mixture into the flour mixture to form a batter. Stir the carrot, celery, tuna, and lemon juice into the batter.

Heat the oil in a skillet. When hot, add spoonfuls of the batter to the skillet and cook over a medium heat until golden on one side. Flip over and cook on the other side. Place the fritters on a platter and keep warm while cooking the remaining batter. Serve with a lemon wedge.

QUINOA, EGGPLANT, AND FRIED EGGS

SERVES 4

This filling, savory breakfast recipe is a balanced, low-FODMAP meal, and it can use up leftover cooked quinoa and low-FODMAP vegetables. Prepare the egg in your favorite way: fry it, poach it, or even scramble it right in the vegetable-and-quinoa mixture.

1 cup (173 g) uncooked quinoa

1 tablespoon (15 ml) light olive oil

1 leek, finely chopped (green parts only)

¼ stalk of celery, finely chopped

1 cup (82 g) diced eggplant

½ cup (25 g) bean sprouts

2 tablespoons (30 ml) soy sauce

½ tablespoon (8 ml) fish sauce

4 eggs

Salt and pepper

Cook the quinoa as per the package instructions. Drain and set aside.

Heat the oil in a skillet or wok. Add the leek and celery and cook for 2 minutes. Add the eggplant and cook for 3 to 4 minutes. Add the cooked quinoa and sauté until the quinoa is browned. Add the bean sprouts and the soy and fish sauces and mix well. Cook the eggs in a little oil in a separate skillet until the whites are cooked but the yolks are still soft. Serve each portion of vegetable-and-quinoa mixture with an egg on top. Season the egg to taste. Serve immediately.

PESTO AND PROSCIUTTO BRUSCHETTA

SERVES 3

Bruschetta is such a simple dish, and it's a crowd-pleaser, too. Serve it as a first course at a dinner party or when friends drop in unexpectedly for drinks and nibbles. This recipe constitutes a complete meal and only takes about 15 minutes to prepare. Just make sure your prosciutto is free from preservatives and other chemicals, which could irritate your digestive system.

6 slices of low-FODMAP bread, each about ¾-inch (2-cm) thick

Olive oil

2 cups (48 g) basil leaves

1½ tablespoons (14 g) pine nuts

1.4 ounces (40 g) Parmesan cheese

1 teaspoon garlic-infused oil (omit for reflux)

Salt

A handful of cherry tomatoes, sliced in half (omit for reflux)

6 slices of prosciutto

Preheat the broiler. Drizzle the bread with olive oil and place under the broiler until toasted on one side. Meanwhile, place the basil, pine nuts, and cheese into a food processor and process until finely chopped. Add all of the garlic oil (if using) and then 1 tablespoon (15 ml) of olive oil at a time until the mixture reaches the right consistency, pulsing in between additions. Season with salt to taste.

Remove the toasted bread from the oven. Spread the pesto on the untoasted side of each piece. Top each with a few cherry tomatoes (if using) and then fold one slice of prosciutto over the tomatoes. Serve immediately.

SALMON, CORN, AND EGGPLANT MUFFINS

MAKES 14 MUFFINS

Two of these savory muffins make a balanced snack. Take a couple with you when you're out and about so that you have a healthy option on hand when hunger strikes. Refrigerate or freeze those you don't eat immediately and then pop them in the microwave for about 20 seconds to reheat them. They're especially delicious warm.

1⅓ cups (210 g) white rice flour

⅓ cup (42 g) tapioca flour

⅓ cup (64 g) potato starch

2 teaspoons (9 g) baking powder

1 teaspoon salt

1 teaspoon ground cumin

1.8 ounces (50 g) butter

1½ cups (123 g) diced eggplant

Kernels from 1 ear of corn

6.5 ounces (185 g) canned salmon

1 egg

1 cup (235 ml) lactose-free milk

Preheat the oven to 350°F (180°C, or gas mark 4). Sift the flours, potato starch, baking powder, salt, and cumin together. Rub the butter into the dry ingredients with clean fingers. Add the eggplant, corn, and salmon and mix. Beat the egg and milk together in a separate bowl and add it to the mixture.

Butter or oil a 14-capacity muffin pan well—gluten-free flours tend to stick. Fill each compartment to the top. Bake for 20 minutes until puffed up and brown on top. Serve warm. Store leftovers in the fridge for 2 to 3 days or freeze for 2 to 3 months.

SALMON DIP

SERVES 6

Laced with parsley and capers, this dip is a balanced snack when it is served with low-FODMAP crackers and vegetable sticks, such as carrots, radishes, fennel, and zucchini. For a little variation, try replacing the salmon with tuna.

10.6 ounces (300 g) canned salmon

17.8 ounces (500 g) cooked potatoes

2 tablespoons (28 g) garlic- and onion-free mayonnaise

3 tablespoons (45 g) plain lactose-free yogurt

2 tablespoons (8 g) finely chopped parsley

1 tablespoon (10 g) capers

Salt and pepper

Place the salmon, potatoes, mayonnaise, yogurt, and parsley into a food processor. Process until well combined and creamy. Mix in the capers and season with salt and pepper. Spoon into a serving bowl and refrigerate for 2 to 3 hours. Store in the fridge for 2 to 3 days.

GINGER COOKIES

MAKES 24 COOKIES

Ginger cookies are classic treats, and you don't need to deprive yourself just because you're eating low-FODMAP. The lemon icing lends them a nice tang, but it can be omitted if you prefer. And you can cut them into any kind of fun shapes, like stars or gingerbread men. Keep them in the fridge for a firmer cookie or on the countertop for a softer one.

For the cookies

1½ cups (237 g) white rice flour

½ cup (64 g) tapioca flour

½ cup (96 g) potato starch

½ teaspoon baking soda

1 tablespoon (6 g) ground gingerroot

1 teaspoon ground cinnamon

1 cup (225 g) brown sugar

5 ounces (150 g) butter, cubed

1 egg, beaten

1 tablespoon (20 g) maple syrup
   or golden syrup

For the icing

1 pasteurized egg white

1½ cups (180 g) confectioners' sugar

1 teaspoon lemon juice

Preheat the oven to 350°F (180°C, or gas mark 4). Line two baking sheets with parchment paper. Place all the dry ingredients in a food processor and process to combine. Add the butter and pulse until fine breadcrumbs are formed. Add the egg and maple syrup and process again. If the dough is sticky, add a little more rice flour until it forms a workable dough. Wrap in plastic wrap and refrigerate for 30 minutes.

Roll out the dough between two sheets of parchment paper until about ¼-inch (5 mm) thick.

Using a round cookie cutter or an upturned glass, cut out circles and place them on the baking sheets. Form the leftover dough into a ball and reroll and repeat, cutting out until the dough is used up. Bake for 8 minutes until golden brown. Cool on a wire rack.

To prepare the icing, beat the egg white until frothy. Fold in the sugar and then add the lemon juice. Drizzle across the cooled cookies with a spoon. Store in an airtight container for 2 to 3 days or freeze for 2 to 3 months.

RHUBARB AND BANANA MUFFINS

MAKES 16 MUFFINS

The creamy sweetness of the bananas and the sharp tang of the rhubarb contrast so well in these light, tasty muffins. You could use an alternative low-FODMAP fruit such as strawberries instead of the rhubarb, if you prefer. Stick to one muffin per serving; freeze most of the batch and defrost them one by one to keep from overindulging.

1¼ cups (250 g) white sugar

1¼ cups (295 ml) light olive oil

4 eggs

1 teaspoon vanilla extract

1⅓ cups (210 g) white rice flour

⅓ cup (42 g) tapioca flour

⅓ cup (64 g) potato starch

1 teaspoon baking powder

1 teaspoon baking soda

1½ cups (183 g) sliced rhubarb

1 large just ripe banana, sliced

Preheat oven to 350°F (180°C, or gas mark 4). Grease a 16-cup muffin pan. Beat the sugar, oil, eggs, and vanilla together. Sift all the dry ingredients together in a separate bowl. Add the rhubarb and banana to the dry ingredients. Gently blend the wet ingredients with the dry. Do not overmix.

Spoon the mixture into the muffin cups, filling each cup full. Bake for 20 minutes or until a skewer inserted into a muffin comes out clean. Cover with aluminum foil during baking if you see that the tops are browning too fast. Turn out onto a cooling rack. When cool, store in an airtight container for 2 to 3 days or freeze for 2 to 3 months.

BANANA, KIWI, AND COCONUT LOAF

SERVES 12

Packed with tropical fruit, this sweet, moist loaf cake is perfect for your morning or afternoon snack. It's so good that you'll definitely be tempted to eat too much of it, so slice it up as soon as it's cool and freeze the individual slices. When it's snack time, place it in the microwave for 10 to 15 seconds, and it'll taste like it just came out of the oven.

WEEK SIX
Sweet Treats

1 just ripe banana

1 medium potato, boiled and mashed

2 ounces (60 ml) melted unsalted butter

1 teaspoon vanilla extract

2 eggs

2 tablespoons (22 g) chia seeds

⅔ cup (104 g) white rice flour

¼ cup (32 g) tapioca flour

¼ cup (48 g) potato starch

1 teaspoon ground allspice

1 teaspoon baking powder

½ teaspoon baking soda

½ cup (100 g) white sugar

½ cup (42 g) shredded coconut

Pinch of salt

1 cup (178 g) chopped kiwi

Preheat the oven to 350°F (180°C, or gas mark 4). In a food processor, blend the banana, potato, butter, and vanilla. Add the eggs and blend again.

Sift together all the dry ingredients except the sugar and coconut. Then, add the sugar and coconut. Add the dry ingredients to the wet and mix well. Add the kiwifruit and mix gently. Pour the mixture into a lined loaf pan and bake for 1 hour. Let the cake stand in the pan for 5 to 10 minutes before removing. Let cool completely before slicing. Store in an airtight container in the fridge for 2 to 3 days or freeze for 2 to 3 months.

CARROT AND PUMPKIN SOUP

SERVES 4 TO 6

Colorful soups like this one are great winter warmers, but you have to be careful not to eat too much because of the high concentration of vegetables in most soups. Always take care that your portion size does not include more vegetables than you would have eaten if you were consuming them separately. Serve this with a protein of your choice.

1 tablespoon (14 g) butter

2 tablespoons (30 ml) light olive oil

1 teaspoon garlic-infused oil
    (omit for reflux)

1 spring onion, finely sliced (green part only)

½ stalk of celery, finely chopped

1 teaspoon ground gingerroot

1 teaspoon ground cumin

1 teaspoon ground coriander

2 teaspoons (4 g) ground turmeric

2 carrots, peeled and chopped

½ pumpkin, peeled and chopped

2 cups (500 ml) garlic- and onion-free
    vegetable stock

1 cup (235 ml) lactose-free milk

5.3 ounces (150 g) fresh corn

1 handful of baby spinach

3.5 ounces (100 g) feta cheese

2 tablespoons (14 g) toasted almond slivers

Chopped fresh cilantro

Smoked paprika

1 bag (7 ounces, or 200 g) of plain
    corn chips

Place the butter, olive oil, and garlic oil (if using) in a large saucepan and heat. Add the spring onion and celery and cook for about 2 to 3 minutes. Add the ginger, cumin, coriander, and turmeric. Continue to cook for about 2 minutes. Add the carrots and pumpkin and cook for 3 to 5 minutes, coating them in the spice mixture. Cover with the stock and boil until the vegetables are soft.

Blend the soup with an immersion blender and then return to the heat and add the milk and corn. Once the soup is heated through, add the spinach and let it wilt in the hot soup. Spoon into bowls and top each with feta, almond slivers, cilantro, and a sprinkle of paprika. Arrange corn chips around the edge of each bowl. Serve immediately. Store leftover soup (without the garnishes) in the fridge for 2 to 3 days or freeze for 2 to 3 months.

TOFU TACOS

SERVES 4

If you're a vegetarian who loves Mexican food, you have to try this quick low-FODMAP weeknight meal. If you have reflux, avoid the tomatoes and use ½ cup (60 g) of zucchini or 1 grated carrot per serving. Have one taco per sitting—and be sure to reserve an extra one for tomorrow's lunch.

1 tablespoon (15 ml) light olive oil

1 block (14 ounces, or 400 g) tofu, chopped into cubes

3 teaspoons (about 7 g) garlic- and onion-free Mexican spice seasoning

4 corn taco shells

3 tomatoes, diced (omit for reflux)

Grated mature cheese

2 cups (110 g) salad leaves

Heat the oil in a skillet and sauté the tofu cubes until browned. Sprinkle the spice seasoning over the cooked tofu, stir well, and cook for 3 to 4 minutes more. Heat the taco shells according to the package instructions. Pile the tofu into the shells and top with tomatoes (if using) and grated cheese. Serve with a little green salad on the side.

GREEK LAMB SALAD

SERVES 4

This salad is a complete meal in itself, and it's pretty enough to serve to guests, too. If you have reflux, replace the tomatoes and bell pepper with 2 radishes and ½ cup (44 g) of sliced fennel. If you don't have time to make pesto, don't worry. You can replace it with a simple dressing of olive oil and fresh lemon juice.

For the salad

Zest of ½ a lemon

1 teaspoon dried thyme

Salt and pepper

14 ounces (400 g) lamb steak

1 red bell pepper (omit for reflux)

1 tomato, sliced (omit for reflux)

1 tablespoon (6 g) chopped mint

5.3 ounces (150 g) feta, cubed

½ cup (50 g) black olives

3 ounces (85 g) arugula

For the dressing

4 tablespoons low-FODMAP pesto (homemade with garlic-infused oil: see the Bruschetta recipe on page 190)

2 tablespoons (30 ml) lemon juice

1 tablespoon (15 ml) olive oil

Mix together the lemon zest, thyme, salt, and pepper and rub it into the steaks. Place on a hot grill and sear for a couple minutes on each side to "seal" the meat. Remove it from the grill while the meat is still pink on the inside. Let the meat rest for 10 minutes and then slice into pieces ½-inch (1.25 cm) thick.

Carefully place the bell pepper (if using) on an open flame and turn constantly until the skin is blackened all over. (Alternatively, blacken the pepper by placing it under the broiler.) Let cool, rub off the skin, and slice into strips.

Lay the pepper, tomato (if using), mint, feta, and olives over the arugula on a large platter and top with the lamb. Combine the pesto, lemon juice, and olive oil to make a dressing. Drizzle the dressing over the platter (or toss the salad in a bowl to combine all ingredients with the dressing).

SHRIMP AND KALE POLENTA

SERVES 4

Polenta soaks up tasty juices well, so it's a good companion for stews or any dish that includes a little sauce. You can have 1 cup (250 g) of cooked polenta because it's made from corn, and cooking polenta with milk instead of water makes it especially creamy. You could use bok choy or spinach instead of the kale, but have no more than ⅓ cup (60 g) of it once cooked.

For the polenta

4 cups (940 ml) lactose-free milk

1 tablespoon (15 ml) light olive oil

2 teaspoons (10 ml) garlic-infused olive oil
   (omit for reflux)

1⅓ cups (188 g) instant polenta

Salt and black pepper

For the kale

2 teaspoons (10 ml) light olive oil

4 cups (268 g) kale

For the shrimp

1 tablespoon (14 g) butter

2 teaspoons (10 ml) light olive oil

1 red chile, deseeded and finely
   chopped (omit for reflux)

1 teaspoon grated gingerroot

16 ounces (450 g) shrimp, peeled and
   trimmed

1 tablespoon (1 g) chopped cilantro

Salt and pepper

First, prepare the polenta. Heat the milk, olive oil, and garlic oil (if using) in a saucepan until almost boiling. Add the polenta gradually, stirring all the time. Bring to a boil and then reduce the heat to low and cook, stirring, for 3 minutes. Remove from the heat and season to taste. Spoon onto plates.

Then prepare the kale. Heat the oil in a skillet and add the kale. Cook until just wilted and pile on top of the polenta.

To prepare the shrimp, heat the butter and oil. Add the chile (if using) and ginger. Cook for 1 minute. Add the shrimp and toss in the oil mixture until cooked. Sprinkle with the cilantro and toss together. Season to taste. Place the shrimp on top of the kale with the juices. Serve hot.

SPICY POTATO PIE

SERVES 4

This recipe's presentation is elegant enough to serve to guests, and it's a complete meal in itself—no side dishes necessary. You can swap the spinach for kale or bok choy, or use a ½ cup (60 g) of zucchini in place of the bell peppers if you have reflux. Have no more than a quarter of the recipe at a sitting.

1 tablespoon (15 ml) light olive oil

2 teaspoons (10 ml) garlic-infused oil (omit for reflux)

1 red chile, finely chopped (omit for reflux)

1 spring onion, chopped (green parts only)

4 slices of bacon

4 potatoes

1 red bell pepper, finely chopped (omit for reflux)

5 ounces (140 g) baby spinach leaves, chopped into fine strips

4 eggs

8 teaspoons (26 g) white rice flour

8 teaspoons (21 g) tapioca flour

Salt and pepper

Preheat the oven to 350°F (180°C, or gas mark 4). Heat the olive oil and garlic oil (if using) in a skillet. Cook the chile (if using) and spring onion until soft. Add the bacon and cook. Then, chop into bite-sized pieces.

Peel and grate the potatoes and squeeze out all excess liquid. Mix all the ingredients together in a large bowl. Oil a 10-inch (26 cm) tart pan and then pour the mixture in and flatten the top. Bake in the oven for about 30 minutes or until set. Store leftovers in the fridge for 2 to 3 days.

ROAST TURKEY WITH STUFFING

SERVES 12 TO 15

Turkey is a holiday staple in many Western countries, and there are lots of ways to prepare it. This method will prevent the turkey from burning during roasting and keeps it moist, juicy, and delicious. Cooking the stuffing separately means that the inside of the turkey will cook more evenly.

For the glaze

Rind and juice of 2 oranges

1 tablespoon (20 g) maple syrup
   or golden syrup

1 tablespoon (15 ml) fish sauce

For the turkey

1 whole turkey, about 10 to 12 pounds
   (4.5 to 5.4 kg)

⅔ cup (80 g) dried cranberries

1 heaped (3 g) tablespoon fresh thyme

1 heaped tablespoon (2 g) fresh rosemary

Pinch of nutmeg

Salt and pepper to taste

4 tablespoons (56 g) softened butter

For the stuffing

6 tablespoons (84 g) butter

2 teaspoons (10 ml) garlic-infused oil
   (omit for reflux)

1 leek, chopped (green parts only)

6 slices of bacon

½ loaf of low-FODMAP bread

3 tablespoons (8 g) finely chopped thyme

3 tablespoons (8 g) finely chopped sage

3 tablespoons (6 g) finely chopped rosemary

Salt and pepper

Lactose-free milk

First, prepare the glaze. Place all the ingredients in a small saucepan and bring to the boil. Boil rapidly until thickened. Remove from the heat and set aside.

Remove the turkey from the fridge an hour before cooking. Preheat the oven to its highest temperature—about 500°F (250°C, or gas mark 10). Place the cranberries, herbs, nutmeg, salt, pepper, and butter into a food processor and grind to a paste. Slowly release the skin over the breast of the turkey from the flesh underneath and spoon the processed mixture underneath and massage into place. Skewer the opening shut.

Truss the turkey and rub butter all over it. Place it in a large baking dish and cover with aluminum foil. Place in the oven and reduce the temperature to 350°F (180°C, or gas mark 4). Once an hour, glaze the turkey with the orange glaze. Roast for 3 hours in total and then remove from the oven. Cover the turkey with fresh aluminum foil and wrap in an old towel for 1 hour before serving with baked stuffing.

To prepare the stuffing, heat the butter and garlic oil (if using). Add the leek and bacon. Cook 2 minutes. Place the bread in a food processor and process into chunks. Add the herbs, season to taste, mix well, and moisten with a little milk. Add the leek-and-bacon mixture and combine. Press into a casserole dish and bake at 350°F (180°C, or gas mark 4) for 1 hour. Serve hot with the turkey along with some garlic- and onion-free gravy.

SHEPHERD'S PIE TARTLETS

SERVES 4

This recipe has a few steps, but it's well worth the effort. You could save time by making these miniature shepherd's pies without the pastry bases, but the pastry does give the dish a lovely crunch. Use extra stock instead of the tomatoes if you have reflux. Have one tart per serving and keep one aside for tomorrow's lunch. Eat with a cup of spinach (30 g) or mixed salad leaves (55 g).

For the pastry

4.7 ounces (133 g) white rice flour

0.8 ounces (22 g) tapioca flour

1.6 ounces (45 g) potato starch

Pinch of salt

3.5 ounces (100 g) butter, cut into small pieces

1 medium egg

For the filling

1 tablespoon (15 ml) light olive oil

½ tablespoon (3 g) fennel seeds

10.6 ounces (300 g) ground beef

½ tablespoon (4 g) corn flour, tapioca flour, or gluten-free flour blend

½ cup (117 ml) garlic- and onion-free beef stock or water, divided

1 tablespoon (4 g) parsley

1 cup (180 g) diced fresh tomatoes (omit for reflux)

For the topping

4 potatoes, cooked until soft

¼ cup (59 ml) lactose-free milk

1 tablespoon (14 g) butter

Salt and pepper

Hard cheese

First, prepare the pastry. Preheat the oven to 350°F (180°C, or gas mark 4). Blend all the dry ingredients in a food processor. Add the butter and process until fine crumbs form. Add the egg and process until the mixture forms a dough. Remove it from the processor and add a little more rice flour if it is too wet (this will depend on the size of your egg). Divide the dough into quarters, press each quarter into a 4- x 4.5-in (11 x 11.5 cm) greased tart pan, and place in the fridge for 30 minutes.

Remove from the fridge, place a circle of parchment paper in the base of each tart, fill with rice or dried beans, and blind bake for 5 minutes. Remove the paper and rice or beans and cook for another 10 minutes. Cover with aluminum foil if the edges start to burn. Remove from the oven and set aside.

Meanwhile, prepare the filling. Heat the oil in a skillet. Add the fennel seeds and cook for 1 minute. Add the ground beef and cook for 5 minutes until browned. Mix the corn flour with a little of the stock in a small bowl. Add it to the meat, along with the parsley, the remaining stock, and the tomatoes (if using). Cook 3 to 4 minutes until the sauce is thickened. Divide evenly between the partially cooked pastry shells.

Finally, prepare the topping. Mash the potatoes with the milk and butter and season to taste. Divide the mash between the tarts, piling it on top of the beef. Grate a little cheese over each and bake in the oven for 20 to 30 minutes or until golden. Serve immediately or let cool and store in the fridge for 1 to 2 days.

CHICKEN AND SPINACH QUICHE

SERVES 4 TO 6

This quiche is perfect for lunch or dinner with friends, and it features a foolproof pastry base that can also be used for tarts and pies. (It's best to press the pastry dough into the tart pan. Rolling it may cause it to break apart because it contains no gluten.) You can use the basic egg-milk mixture in the filling as a template for endless variations, so go ahead and experiment with different proteins and low-FODMAP vegetables.

For the pastry

4.7 ounces (133 g) white rice flour

0.8 ounces (22 g) tapioca flour

1.6 ounces (45 g) potato starch

Pinch of salt

3.5 ounces (100 g) butter, cut into pieces

1 medium egg

For the filling

2 eggs

6.8 ounces (200 ml) lactose-free milk

1 tablespoon (3 g) fresh thyme leaves

Salt and pepper

1 cup (140 g) chopped cooked chicken

2 cups (60 g) baby spinach

1 cup (120 g) grated mature cheese

Additional thyme for serving

First, prepare the pastry. Preheat the oven to 350°F (180°C, or gas mark 4). Blend all the dry ingredients in a food processor. Add the butter and process until fine crumbs form. Add the egg and process until the mixture forms a dough. Remove it from the processor and add a little more rice flour if it is too wet (this will depend on the size of your egg). Press the dough into a greased 10-inch (26 cm) tart pan and place in the fridge for 30 minutes. Remove from the fridge, place a circle of parchment paper in the base of the tart, fill with rice or dried beans, and blind bake for 5 minutes. Remove the paper and rice or beans and cook for another 5 minutes. Remove from the oven and set aside.

Meanwhile, prepare the filling. Beat the eggs and milk together. Add the thyme and season to taste. Scatter the chicken over the pastry base. Cover with the spinach leaves and press down a little (the spinach will wilt quickly once heated). Sprinkle the grated cheese over top and then add the milk mixture. Bake for 20 to 25 minutes until the filling is set. Serve with a sprinkling of fresh thyme leaves.

DIARY PAGE | **WEEK SIX** | DATE ___/___/___

SLEEP _____ hours   from _____ to _____

Quality of sleep _____

_____

RELAXATION _____ minutes   from _____ to _____

Type _____

_____

EXERCISE _____ minutes   from _____ to _____

Type _____

_____

TIME FOR SELF _____ minutes   from _____ to _____

Type _____

_____

FAMILY TIME _____ minutes   from _____ to _____

Type _____

_____

PRODUCTIVE TIME _____ minutes   from _____ to _____

Type _____

_____

BOWEL MOVEMENTS _____ number   times _____

Type* _____

_____

MEDICATION

Type _____   _____

_____   _____

SUPPLEMENTS

Type _____   _____

_____   _____

*To find what type of bowel movement you've had, search the Internet for "Bristol Stool Chart."

FOOD JOURNAL | WEEK SIX

MEAL	TIME	NOTES/SYMPTOMS
Breakfast		
Morning snack		
Lunch		
Afternoon snack		
Dinner		

Lifestyle Exercise:
PRODUCTIVE WORK

Productive work is essential. It makes us feel that our lives are worthwhile and that our time spent has been well spent—and not just frittered away by staring at or playing with electronic devices. When you spend time productively, you have something to show for your efforts. A closet has been cleared out and looks wonderfully tidy. Or, you've sewn your daughter's ballet tutu and she is thrilled with it. Or, you've made a batch of low-FODMAP muffins in preparation for the week to come.

Work is at its most productive when it aligns with what you want from life. If everything you do has an overall philosophy of life behind it or a goal at the end of it, then the work feels joyous and satisfying.

Know who you are, sort your priorities, and find out what you truly want from life—and the rest will follow.

WHAT CONSTITUTES PRODUCTIVE TIME?

Here are a few of the many activities that the term "productive time" encompasses.

MAKING MONEY

Of course, working at a job is a way to make money—but what if you are a stay-at-home mother or a student? Not everyone has a full-time job outside the home. So, making a bit of extra money always feels really productive. Think about your skills and hobbies and see if you can earn a little income from them. Are you great at baking and decorating cakes? Writing? Catering? Making teddy bears?

PROPERTY PRUNING

Property pruning means tossing all the excess stuff you own and never use. The English writer and artist William Morris said, "Have nothing in your house that you do not know to be useful, or believe to be beautiful," and I bet you can't say that's completely true of your home. So, move through your house, one room and one cupboard at a time, and toss or give away anything you haven't used in the last year. Remember that you don't own your property: your property owns you.

ANSWERING YOUR MAIL

Go through all of those emails in your inbox and respond to them, delete them, or pop them in a folder for future reference. And tackle that pile of paper mail on your kitchen counter. After it's all cleared away, you'll have taken a load off your mind and you'll feel much lighter.

PHONING YOUR FRIENDS

Call a few of the people you've been meaning to get in touch with but somehow never find the time to contact. That's another weight off your mind.

CROSSING ONE THING OFF YOUR TO-DO LIST

Think about what you can actually do on that long, long list of must-dos. If you have half an hour to spare before your next appointment or before picking up the kids from school, don't waste it. Instead, spend it on a job that will take less than thirty minutes to finish. Won't you feel good on your way to your next mission?

HOW DO YOU BECOME HIGHLY PRODUCTIVE?

It *is* possible! Here's how:

- **Say no.** First and foremost, learn to say no! We waste so much time taking care of things for other people—things that they are more than capable of doing themselves. No, you can't take your teenage daughter to her friend's house when she can get the bus. No, you won't join the committee for the local tennis club just because you play there occasionally. No, you won't have coffee with an acquaintance so she can pick your brain for free for ideas related to your business.

- **Get up early.** Go to bed earlier so you can get up earlier. You will be much more productive in the morning than you are at night after a long, busy day.

- **Get help.** Don't do all the menial jobs just because you can. If you can afford it, get someone to clean your house to free you up for more meaningful productive work.

- **Exercise self-discipline.** Check your email only a few times a day at specific times and turn off your computer or log out of your email in between. Interrupting yourself constantly will reduce the quality of your productive time.

- **Make a to-do list** . . . but put only three things on it each day. A list will help clear your mind, but things will plague you if they stay on it too long. Once in a while you should scrap your list and start again. Do the biggest, most important task first, not the smallest and easiest. Even if you only manage to do one of the bigger jobs in a day, you will feel far more productive than if you had done three smaller jobs.

- **Be productive, not busy.** What's the difference? "Busy" is that overwhelmed, scatter-brained feeling. "Productive" gives you a sense of accomplishment. Cut out the busyness and focus on being productive.

Your Exercise This Week:
ONE HOUR EVERY DAY

- Work out what is important to you.

- Shape your productive time around this.

- Get up an hour earlier than you need to.

- Turn off your phone and emails.

- Write three things only on your to-do list, making sure that at least one of them is aligned with your life goals.

- Complete the most important task first.

Diet Integration:

DEALING WITH COWORKERS

The way in which you deal with your coworkers—both generally and with regard to your IBS—depends on your personality. Some people are very private and will probably never reveal something as personal as an intolerance diet. Others prefer to have matters out in the open and choose to talk about their issues with coworkers. That's a personal choice, but either way, you must always, always stand up for yourself and your health.

WHAT TO EAT FOR LUNCH AT WORK

The best lunch solution is leftovers from the dinner recipes in this book. That way, you can be sure you are eating low-FODMAP food. So, when you prepare dinner, put aside your lunch portion before serving dinner: Don't wait to see if there are leftovers.

If it happens that you have nothing left over and you have run out of alternatives, there is usually a sushi shop nearby in towns and cities, but you'll have to steer clear of avocado or mashed up fish (which could contain onion or garlic). Even though many cafés have gluten-free food these days, gluten-free food is not necessarily low-FODMAP. In fact, many gluten-free baked goods are made from almond flour, which is not safe for IBS sufferers.

SNACKS AT WORK

Your meal plans tell you what to take to work for snacks, but just in case you forget, keep a packet of plain rice crackers and some low-FODMAP nuts or a jar of peanut butter in your desk drawer.

WORK LUNCHES AND BREAKFASTS

This will be a challenge, and people who have been open about their diet among their coworkers will be in a better position to insist on getting something low-FODMAP to eat. You can always call the café or restaurant in advance and have a chat with the chef. Otherwise, you'll have to eat whatever you can and have a stash of backup food brought from home which you can eat afterwards. It might also be a good idea to have a small snack before arriving so that you are not tempted to eat something that will hurt you.

BIRTHDAY CAKES

In office workplaces, it seems, birthdays always have to be celebrated with cakes. If you know that a birthday is coming up, bring one of your sweet treats with you so that you don't miss out on the fun. This will be a real test of your resolve during the elimination stage of the diet—but stay strong. During the reintroduction stage, you may find you have no problem with wheat and lactose, and so cakes will be permitted again.

ROBERT

Robert was in a severe emotional slump when he first contacted me. His IBS had started when his partner was diagnosed with cancer and he left his job to take care of her. Even though the cancer went into remission after many grueling months and his wife felt strong enough to return to work, Robert stayed at home because his IBS symptoms were so debilitating. He felt completely burned out and had no energy to do anything but watch television from his comfy chair.

I started him on the low-FODMAP diet and we worked hard on getting his sleep patterns normalized so he could support the diet with restful sleep. By the end of week two, Robert's energy levels were up, his symptoms had disappeared, and he was sleeping well. Before, he had been content to do very little all day, but now, he really felt the lack of productive work in his life. During one of our weekly phone calls, I mentioned the possibility of going back to work on a part-time basis, but he had

decided that he didn't want to return to the same high-powered corporate job. I suggested that he look in the paper for a local part-time job, and he said he would never find anything nearby in his field. I explained that for now, the kind of work he did wasn't as important as simply getting out of the house.

Robert got up early the next day and headed for the shops to get the local paper. He immediately applied for several part-time jobs and within a few days had a job as an assistant to the local butcher. During our next call, he laughed at how life turns out. He would never have dreamed that one day he would be working in a butcher's shop. He started the job during the last week of the program and was bubbling with energy at finally having a purpose to his days. In just six weeks, he had been transformed from a burned-out person suffering from daily IBS symptoms to a gainfully employed man who sprang out of bed each day, excited to have his life back.

Conclusion
The Joy of Transformation

You've made it! You have finished the six-week program. Now it's time to reintegrate all the food groups and individual foods that you didn't react to in order to create a perfect final diet for you as an individual. This is your lifetime diet. It will be different from anyone else's, and it will keep you symptom-free. Of course, this doesn't constitute a cure: IBS is waiting just around the corner for you to slip up, but now you have control over your symptoms, not vice versa.

We're all human, so it's natural to fall off the wagon every now and then, but the difference is that now you know how to get back on it. Yes, you will suffer for a couple of days, but then all will be well in your world again. And the longer you do this, the more determined you will be to stay on the straight and narrow. The symptoms really aren't worth a slipup, but don't beat yourself up if you do make a mistake.

However, do take care that one thing doesn't lead to another until you find that you constantly have symptoms again. This can happen so gradually that you might not really notice at first—until one day you feel so bad that you can't ignore your symptoms any longer. If that happens, go back to week 1 of this program and start again.

Maintain all the new habits you have formed. Continue to have five small meals a day, approximately three hours apart. Never overload your digestive system, but never starve it, either. Sleep eight hours a night within the routine you have established in order to support the diet. Continue doing the breathing exercise several times a day for the rest of your life to keep your stress levels manageable. Exercise daily for a healthy body and mind. Treat yourself and your family like the jewels they are. Be creative and productive. Craft a life that you love that is filled with joy.

References and Resources

WEBSITES

MONASH UNIVERSITY RESEARCH CENTRE

Monash created the low-FODMAP diet. I highly recommend both their app and their booklet, both of which can be found on their website. Their blog is great for up-to-date IBS and low-FODMAP research, suggestions, and recipes.
www.monashfodmap.com

KATE SCARLATA

Kate is a registered dietitian and low-FODMAP diet educator. Her site is a great place for accurate information on the low-FODMAP diet and includes her own findings from dealing with IBS patients in her practice.
www.katescarlata.com

FOODS

CASA DE SANTE

Stocks a wide range of low-FODMAP foods, including spice mixtures, snack packs, drinks, stock, teas, and salad dressings.
www.casadesante.com

FODY FOODS

Stocks a wide range of low-FODMAP foods, including snack bars, sauces, salsas, stock, snack packs, cereals, chips, and seasonings.
www.fodyfoods.com

TRUESELF

Low-FODMAP snack bars developed by Dr. Miechelle O'Brien, a practicing gastroenterologist who is passionate about helping IBS sufferers.
www.trueselffoods.com

RESEARCH

MICHIGAN MEDICINE, UNIVERSITY OF MICHIGAN

"Study: Low FODMAP Diet Improves Quality of Life for IBS Patients"
labblog.uofmhealth.org/lab-report/study-low-fodmap-diet-improves-quality-of-life-for-ibs-patients

About the Author

SUZANNE PERAZZINI lives in New Zealand in a house overlooking the Pacific Ocean with her husband. She is a nutritional therapist specializing in IBS and the low-FODMAP diet, a qualified teacher, an award-winning author, and a fulltime low-FODMAP diet coach. Her website, www.strandsofmylife.com, features low-FODMAP recipes, videos, and articles on IBS and the diet. She has been featured on numerous podcasts, has had articles on several large health websites, and had many of her recipes published in a variety of magazines. She has suffered from IBS forever, and after having her life transformed by the low-FODMAP diet, she now dedicates her days to coaching others on how to eliminate their IBS symptoms once and for all.

She helps people change their lives every day through her coaching work. Her greatest moments have been turning a 3-year-old girl from a child curled up in the corner in pain to a happy child playing out in the yard with her friends and helping an 83-year-old woman, who had suffered horribly all her life, discover that there is peace on earth after all. She would love you to become another of her success stories through the guidance in this book.

Index